A SPIRITUAL
FIELD GUIDE

A SPIRITUAL
FIELD GUIDE

Meditations for the Outdoors

BERNARD BRADY
AND MARK NEUZIL

BrazosPress
Grand Rapids, Michigan

© 2005 by Bernard Brady and Mark Neuzil

Published by Brazos Press
a division of Baker Publishing Group
P.O. Box 6287, Grand Rapids, MI 49516-6287

Printed in the United States of America

Library of Congress Cataloging-in-Publication Data
Brady, Bernard V. (Bernard Vincent), 1957–
    A spiritual field guide : meditations for the outdoors / Bernard Brady and Mark Neuzil.
        p.   cm.
    Includes bibliographical references and index.
    ISBN 1-58743-118-1 (pbk.)
    1. Nature—Religious aspects—Christianity—Meditations. I. Neuzil, Mark. II. Title.
BT695.5.B725 2005
242—dc22   2004023980

To our families

Contents

Introduction

At the very beginning of Herman Melville's classic book *Moby Dick*, the character Ishmael reflects on the power of water on the human spirit. He describes how every Sunday afternoon scores of "inlanders"—"water-gazers" he calls them—gather to stare at the ocean. "They must get just as nigh the water as they possibly can without falling in. And there they stand," he says. "Say you are in the country; in some high land of lakes. Take almost any path you please, and ten to one it carries you down in a dale, and leaves you there by a pool in the stream. There is magic in it. . . . Yes, as every one knows, meditation and water are wedded for ever."[1] We, the authors of this book, think Ishmael is correct; meditation and water are wedded . . . forever. And we think meditation is also wedded to forests and to mountains and to the sight of a soaring eagle and perhaps (at least for one of us) even to the buzzing of mosquitoes. Some "thing" in nature or some "thing" about nature draws us out of ourselves and invites us to sit, stare, relax, and, often, pray. For us this "thing" is God. God's fingerprints, God's breath, and God's intentions are in and through the natural world.

Every year, millions of people explore their natural surroundings by walking in parks, climbing mountains, watching birds at a backyard feeder, camping in forests, or floating down a river. Millions of people get down on their knees and pull weeds from their gardens, notice all sorts of creepy-crawly bugs, are amazed every year by the details of a flower, and wonder at the determination of seeds as they push up through hard ground. Like Ishmael's "water-gazers" they enjoy simply sitting by a lake, or looking out from a hillside, or swinging in a hammock. For many people, such experiences are occasions to contemplate sacred things. If you are one of those people, this book is for you.

We love wilderness. We love it for its beauty, power, and majesty. Others can stand at the foot of a great sculpture or near a painting or can hear a sonata and find the results of God at work through the efforts of humans. We rest between the gunwales of our canoe at a quiet bay on a Canadian shield lake, watching the loons or a bear, smelling the white cedar trees and the tamarack swamp, and see evidence of a divine hand. "Never have my thoughts been more devoutly raised to heaven," wrote

10

Priscilla Wakefield in the early nineteenth century, "than in some of our rambles through these magnificent forests; especially of an evening, when we have prepared our bed of dried leaves, under the canopy of a branching oak, or a lofty pine; the moon's silver rays casting a modest light through the trees, the whip-poor-will lulling us with his melancholy note to sleep; assisted by the lowing of distant herds of cattle, or the shrill whooping of the crane."[2]

In 1844, Edinburgh journalist and amateur naturalist Robert Chambers, anticipating Charles Darwin by nearly a decade, wrote *Vestiges of the Natural History of Creation*.[3] In his controversial book, Chambers (who published it anonymously to protect himself from criticism) examined the natural history of the world as a way to understand God, while at the same time wondering if or how the geologic record squared with the biblical accounts of creation. Although he thought the Bible contained faults regarding the ways of the physical world, Chambers provided those "natural philosophers" of his day who believed both in the Almighty and in the power of science a reason to continue their work. To Chambers, the study of nature was, as Kenneth R. Miller put it, "akin to the worship of God."[4]

Nineteenth-century writers like Wakefield and Chambers helped make popular the subject of the relationship between God and nature. By the twentieth century, it was common for writers to muse on the spiritual and the sublime. Flannery O'Connor, for example, expressed the view of many contemporary people when she wrote, "For me, the visible universe is a reflection of the invisible universe."[5] It is not our goal in this book to produce, or reproduce, our own experiences with the spiritual world while journeying through the natural one. It is rather to invite you to read and mull over some texts or musings—some classic, some obscure—about the visible universe that reflect the invisible universe.

As the psalmist proclaims, there is an order in nature, and, according to our plan, there is an order to this book. It has five thematic chapters: "On Creation and the Creator," "Our Place in Creation," "That Special Spot," "Into the Wilderness," and "All God's Creatures." Each chapter contains many short excerpts and quotations exploring its particular theme. Each also includes an introductory essay that provides some context for understanding the selections. These introductions include commentary, explanation, and background information on each reading.

Many of the selections are taken from Christian scripture. Frankly, as we prepared and researched this book, the number of biblical references to nature surprised us. The book also includes many commentators representing every era in Christian history as well as many denominations. We expanded our selection to include authors influenced by the Christian tradition as well as some decidedly non-Christian sources. The book is ecumenical in that it invites consideration from a wide range of religious voices around a consistent theme. We have found all of these sources inspiring or interesting.

How to Read This Book

It is rare for authors to suggest how their book ought to be read. We have some ideas. Certainly, you are free to read this book in the way that people normally read books—begin on page 1 and move through the text at an efficient and economical speed so as to complete it within a reasonable amount of time. May we suggest an alternative way to read? We encourage you to slow down and purposefully read this book.

Each selection is short and can be read within a few minutes. This is not to say, however, that each section ought to be read as quickly as possible. Read slowly. Read carefully. One of us enjoys reading the selections out loud (even though his kids think that is weird), because that helps him to better "hear" the words. Our hope is that you read not simply to get *through* this book, but to get *into* this book.

Luke Dysinger offers some helpful advice for spiritual reading. His comments are influenced by the ancient Christian tradition of contemplative praying of scripture. He reminds us that God's voice, God's words, can enter our lives in many ways. Often, God's voice comes to us like it came to the prophet Elijah, as a faint sound. As

Elijah had to listen, so must we. This is not easy. Indeed, there is perhaps no more difficult place than the contemporary world, with its many, many distractions, to listen for the voice of God. Dysinger suggests that when you begin contemplation on spiritual texts, you should "place yourself in a comfortable position and allow yourself to become silent."[6]

One of our spiritual/naturalist mentors, Sigurd Olson, has similar advice. Olson is often identified with Listening Point, a favorite location of his in the north woods of Minnesota. In his book of the same name, he writes, "Each time I have gone there I have found something new which has opened up great realms of thought and interest. . . . From it I have seen the immensity of space and glimpsed at times the grandeur of creation."[7] He continues, "I named this place Listening Point because only when one comes to listen, only when one is aware and still, can things be seen and heard. Everyone has a listening-point somewhere. It does not have to be in the north or close to the wilderness, but some place of quiet where the universe can be contemplated with awe."[8] Following the suggestions of Dysinger and Olson, we invite you to search for moments of silence in the woods, along a river, or in your backyard (an easy chair will also do) as you read selections from this book.

Dysinger's first recommendation is that you read a spiritual text slowly. In fact, he says you should read it gently. He writes, "Savor each portion of the reading, constantly listening for the 'still, small voice' of a word or phrase."[9] If an idea or word or phrase captures your attention, repeat it to yourself. Let the word or phrase roll through your mind. Come back to it and recall it later in the day. Another writer on spiritual reading, M. Basil Pennington, captures a link between words and God as he writes, "'Through Him all things were made.' The whole of creation bespeaks of its Maker. As the Greeks would say, the whole of creation is full of *logoi*, 'little words,' that give expression to the Logos, the Word." Dysinger suggests that after interacting with the word or phrase, you should speak to God. "Give to God what you have found in your heart."[10] Then pause for a moment.

Do not feel confined to read the book from beginning to end. Start with a theme that interests you or read the texts randomly. While the selections fit into general themes, each can stand on its own. You have our permission to read the selections in any order you wish! Like the voice of the child that Augustine heard in the garden, we say, "Pick up and read . . . pick up and read." Take a moment, open the book up, and read.

If you are in a group, have someone read an introduction and share that information with others. The recommended readings come from all over the book; look for ways to tie them together—common ideas or themes,

15

similar subject matter—and also look for ways they are different. Think about it. Talk about it.

The book can be used as a backpacker's companion—that's how we use it—or as a volume to take to a summer cabin; it can be read aloud to a large group or pondered on a park bench. Carry it as part of your journey.

Reading Plans

Here are a few plans to help the ambitious reader map out a literary journey to accompany a longer trip or a spell in the backyard hammock. Each daily reading is designed for a morning, noon, and evening meditation.

A. Weeklong Trip I

DAY ONE

Holiness cannot be confined, Wendell Berry, pp. 32–33.

God saw how good it was, Genesis 1:1–25, pp. 33–35

The book of created nature, Augustine of Hippo, p. 44.

DAY TWO

The Breastplate of St. Patrick, Patrick of Ireland, pp. 72–73.

The fragility of humans, Psalm 8:1–9, p. 64.

Environmental Sabbath II, United Nations Environment Programme, p. 72.

DAY THREE

Jesus's places to pray, Mark 1:35; Luke 4:42, p. 93.

The highest mountain, Chief Black Elk, pp. 114–15.

Listen, Thomas Merton, pp. 96–97.

DAY FOUR

Wilderness tests us, Deuteronomy 8:2–10, pp. 129–30.

The call of Elijah, 1 Kings 19:11–12, p. 139.

Connection to nature/connection to the infinite, Barbara Kingsolver, pp. 142–43.

DAY FIVE

Notice the ravens, Luke 12:24–28, p. 163.

Sermon to the birds, St. Francis of Assisi, p. 173.

Epic journey, Aldo Leopold, pp. 166–67.

B. Weeklong Trip II

DAY ONE

Flowers, Thérèse of Lisieux, p. 44.

A place of great meaning, Bernard of Clairvaux, p. 94.

A good person is like a tree planted near water, Psalm 1:3, p. 103.

DAY TWO

Autumn floods, Chuang Tzu, p. 106.

The ark came to rest, Genesis 8:3–4, p. 108.

I give water to my people, Isaiah 43:19–21, p. 105.

DAY THREE

A covenant with all living things, Genesis 9:8–18, p. 159.

Chief Seattle's address, Ted Perry,.pp. 75–76.

Animals know more than we, Isaiah 1:3; Job 12:7–10; Jeremiah 8:7, p. 168.

DAY FOUR

Canticle of the sun, St. Francis of Assisi, pp. 73–74.

Father Zosima, Fyodor Dostoyevsky, p. 77.

Virtuous creatures, Proverbs 30:24–33, p. 169.

DAY FIVE

Holy now, Peter Mayer, pp. 157–58.

Life without meaning, Sigurd Olson, pp. 133–34.

The wolf and the lamb, the calf and the lion, Isaiah 11:6–9, p. 170.

C. Weekend Trip I

DAY ONE

Your works are full of wonder, traditional Jewish prayer, p. 39.

How varied are Your works, Psalm 104:1, 10–28, pp. 35–37.

The whole universe, Thomas Aquinas, p. 42.

DAY TWO

The earth is polluted, Isaiah 24:4–5, p. 76.

The earth belongs to all—not just to the rich, St. Ambrose, pp. 78–79.

A fight over ownership, the Talmud, p. 80.

DAY THREE

Mountains break into song, Isaiah 55:12–13 and 44:23, p. 111.

Majesty of the mountains, Pope John Paul II, p. 115.

Honor the ant, Francis A. Schaeffer, pp. 173–74.

D. Weekend Trip II

DAY ONE

God made it, God loves it, God cares for it, Julian of Norwich, pp. 46–47.

These mountains, Annie Dillard, p. 116.

Though I walk through a dark valley, Psalm 23, pp. 139–40.

Day Two

God's wrath, Isaiah 13:13–14, 21–22, p. 162.

The consequences of original sin, Martin Luther, p. 135.

Catching glimpses of God, Thomas Merton, p. 65.

Day Three

We need to be able to taste grace, Barbara Kingsolver, pp. 143–44.

A lonely spot, Edward Abbey, p. 95.

Share experiences with others, Sigurd Olson, p. 132.

E. Day Trip I

Resurrection, Henry David Thoreau, pp. 163–64.

Contact with nature restores us, Pope John Paul II, pp. 141–42.

Refreshing the soul, Richard Jefferies, pp. 113–14.

F. Day Trip II

Three views from space, astronauts Edgar Mitchell, James Irwin, Gene Cernan, p. 47.

In our image, Genesis 1:26–31, pp. 63–64.

Celtic blessing, Fiona McLeod, p. 116.

G. Backyard Breaks

Sister Cricket and little worms, Thomas of Celaus
pp. 171–72.

God stills the seas, Psalm 65:7–13, pp. 136–37.

The meaning of pasture, Gene Stratton Porter,
p. 140.

Noah sends out the dove, Genesis 8:6–12, p. 158.

We are astonished at tiny ants, Augustine of Hippo,
pp. 38–39.

On nature and the soul, Florence Curl Jones (Puilulimet), p. 132.

1

On Creation and the Creator

Pick up and read . . . pick up and read." These words Augustine, the fourth- and fifth-century church father, heard while he sat in a garden, contemplating his life's direction. These words, perhaps coming from a child in a neighboring garden, encouraged Augustine to take up the Bible. His conversion becomes a paradigm for Christian life and its relationship to nature. While sitting in a garden, pick up and read.

The first section of this book begins with biblical reflections on nature such as those Augustine might have pondered. The preface to the selections from scripture is an interesting thought from Wendell Berry. Called by some "the prophet of rural America," Berry is a farmer, writer, and poet living in Kentucky. He suggests that the Bible is best read outdoors. "We see that the miraculous," he writes, "is not extraordinary, but the common mode of existence."[1] Bring this book outdoors, and in particular read the second selection, the first chapter of Genesis. Look around. Genesis affirms that God created the world you see around you. This world is intrinsically good. Indeed the phrase "and God saw it was good" is repeated seven times in the first chapter of Genesis. Nothing in nature is independent from God, and at the same time no one thing in nature is identifiable with God. We can see God in nature but note that nature is not God.

Those with environmental or conservationist leanings have often made connections with a Supreme Being. If there is a conservationist prayer in the Bible, Psalm 104 is it. Tradition has it that David wrote the Psalms, but recent thinking says that several authors, over several centuries, penned these lyrical works. The ancient reader may have recited the Psalms—hymns of praise and poetic descriptions—and felt reassured by the order of nature and God's continuing care for all things. Read Psalm 104 aloud as your response to what you heard in the first chapter of Genesis and what you see around you. The psalm praises God for the goodness of creation. Creation, moreover, is ordered. There is an interconnectedness to the world. Creation is marked by relationships. The streams, for example, come down from the hills and provide nourishment for birds and animals. The earth provides grass for cows and bread and wine for humans. All creatures, including you, rely on God's mercy and love. It should be impossible to praise God while despoiling the earth.

The Book of Proverbs is part of a group of books in the Old Testament known as "Wisdom Literature." Wisdom is an important theme in the Hebrew scriptures but one that Christians have not tended to pick up on. What is wisdom? How does one become wise? We all know people who are learned yet lack an ability to know the right thing to do in tough situations. We also know people who have little formal education whose opinions we value. The issue is a form of knowing that some people have as a result of experience—wisdom. As the poet Samuel Coleridge put it: "Common sense in an uncommon degree is what the world calls wisdom."[2] The Wisdom books—Proverbs, Job, Psalms, Ecclesiastes, Song of Solomon, Sirach, and Wisdom of Solomon (the latter two are deuterocanonical, accepted by Roman Catholic and Eastern Orthodox churches but not Protestant churches)—aim to develop this very valuable sort of knowledge.

In the Hebrew scriptures wisdom is personified. For example, wisdom is often presented as a woman. God creates her, and as the text suggests, she plays a role in the creation of the world. There is then "wisdom" in nature.

Consider other personifications of wisdom. For one, through the ages Christian theology has often interpreted the image of wisdom in the Old Testament to be Jesus. In another example, in Greek and Roman cultures owls represented wisdom. (In scriptures, owls tend to represent desolation or an ill omen.) Think of their current personas: poised, stately, and vigilant. They sit in trees, all large eyes and bigger heads, examining things around them, as a scholar would. According to other traditions, owls have a sort of inner light that helps them see in the darkness. Wisdom, highly valued in ancient times but perhaps undervalued today, ought to be sought and cultivated in our travels through nature.

When you finish these selections, two things may impress you. First, it seems that the Bible is quite relevant in what it has to say about nature. It provides much-needed food for thought for moderns. Second, there is a huge gap (historical, cultural, political, social, and indeed religious) between ancient times and our own times. Our place within nature is very different from that which our forbearers experienced. Put quite simply, they lived much closer to nature. We have air conditioners, furnaces, bug spray, houses with indoor plumbing, and the Weather Channel to shield us from the threats of nature. And many of us also live in big cities, marked by skyscrapers, smog, and subways, which can keep us from being touched by nature. In most of our daily lives, nature, its beauty, serenity, terror, and power, are many steps removed from our usual paths.

The Beauty of God's Creation

"A divine voice sings through all creation," so the Jewish prayer goes. To see the beauty of God's creation is a way to see the beauty of God. This theme runs through the works of authors like Augustine of Hippo, the writers of Sirach, and Thomas Aquinas.

Augustine of Hippo (354–430) may have been the most influential Christian theologian of all time. Augustine's ideas on such fundamental issues as God, Jesus, love, sin, virtue, war, and sex continue to influence Christians of all denominations today, nearly 1,600 years after his death. Augustine's life, narrated in his autobiography, *The Confessions*, was one of youthful indiscretion and ultimate conversion. As a bishop Augustine was involved in many significant theological disputes and arguments within the growing Christian church. He disagreed with Christians who held that spiritual reality was the "true good" and physical reality—the natural world—was sinful. Augustine argued strenuously against this idea. All creation, he held, in its "depths" was full of the divine presence.

The world is full of traces of God, and indeed creation is a testimony to God's presence. God's power can suddenly appear in a thunderstorm or a cyclone. God's beauty seems obvious in the stars, the trees, the hills, and the sounds of the night. Sometimes it is easy to take for granted what the nature writer Paul Gruchow called "the grace of the wild"; our challenge is to see and appreciate nature, no matter how many times we experience its splendor firsthand.

Augustine points to the two seemingly contradictory Christian ideas about creation. The first is that creation is good "in itself." That is to say, its goodness precedes human nature and human reflection. Creation is good because God said it was good. Augustine tells us that we ought to focus and discipline ourselves so we can see creation as God's work. God is mirrored in the awesome beauty, diversity, and power of creation. The second idea of creation is that it is good "for us." Creation has a utility value for us. Our well-being is dependent on creation—indeed on the well-being of creation. Our very existence relies on clean water and air. Our food, clothing, and sources of shelter all find their sources in God's creation. Examples are all around us: a Douglas fir can be milled into lumber for a new subdivision; a red fox can be trapped, skinned, and tanned into hide for a coat; a brook trout can be hooked, cleaned, and eaten. In this way, a fir tree or a red fox or a brook trout can be appreciated as God's creation. God is their God, too. These two ideas are captured in Genesis when it states that humans were placed in the Garden to "cultivate and care" for it.

Part of the beauty of a sunrise is in the idea that the sun was God's idea. These two notions, the inherent goodness of nature and the usefulness of nature, mix when we address our spiritual concerns. Augustine notes the revitalizing capacity of nature. Noticing the colors, the smells, the sights, the sounds, from tiny ants to great whales, enriches our soul and reminds us of the Creator.

Remind is a key word. Sirach locates God in creation, yet does not limit the being of God to creation. Thomas Aquinas (1225–1274), the famous medieval theologian and philosopher, reflects on the profound goodness of God that, he notes, cannot be captured in any one of God's creatures. Thomas Traherne (1634–1674), an English poet who wrote much about our relationship with God and our closeness to him, is concerned with "enjoying the world aright." As we step back and reflect on the whole of creation, we can sense the awesomeness of the goodness of God.

Knowing God

"How can I know God?" This question has been addressed by great thinkers through history. Augustine and the nineteenth-century French saint Thérèse of Lisieux (1873–1897), among others, give us the image of nature as God's book. We should "pick up and read" nature. The image of nature as a book is an appealing one to the legions of people who live a life of the mind as well as enjoy a walk in the woods. Books about nature have a long and successful history in the marketplace. For example, Izaak Walton (1593–1683) wrote *The Compleat Angler* in 1653 in England; by some counts, Walton's short treatise on life and fishing has gone through more reprinted editions than any other single book outside of the Bible. What is sometimes forgotten is Walton's subtitle: *The Contemplative Man's Recreation,* or the way he weaves the works of God into his text. One of Walton's famous lines is: "I might tell you that Almighty God is said to have spoken to a fish, but never to a beast; that he hath made a whale a ship, to carry and set his prophet, Jonah, safe on the appointed shore."[3] Authors like Walton and others present a way to "read" nature; one of Walton's contemporaries, Daniel Defoe (1660–1731), created one of literature's most memorable characters by juxtaposing civilization and nature while draping a spiritual theme over the tale. Robinson Crusoe thanked God for his "solitary Condition" on the "deserted" island and saw himself as happier than if he had been in the "Pleasures of the World."[4]

Augustine uses the word *confession* in the New Testament sense, meaning a testimony or a declaration of faith.[5] As he says, "So when you praise God, you are confessing to God."[6] Creation confesses to the greatness of God. And God's goodness can be found in all things. The next few selections complement Augustine. A woman who wished to remain anonymous, Julian of Norwich (1342–ca. 1416), was so named because she spent the last twenty years of her life in a small house attached to the church of St. Julian in Norwich, England. She was a mystic; her life was one of meditation, prayer, and advising others in the spiritual life. On May 8, 1373, she received a series of visions, what she referred to as "showings." Julian recorded the visions in her work *Revelations of Divine Love* and in doing so became the first well-known female English writer. Julian lived during dramatic times, including the Hundred Years War and the Black Plague. She herself suffered a life-threatening illness. Yet she writes with enormous confidence in God's presence and enduring love for all creation.

Three astronauts also reflect on a powerful and profound experience that few people have gone through—on seeing earth from space.

On wonder

AUTHOR UNKNOWN

If a dead man is raised to life, all men spring up in astonishment. Yet every day one that had no being is born, and no man wonders, though it is plain to all, without doubt, that it is a greater thing for that to be created which was without being than for that which had being to be restored. Because the dry rod of Aaron budded, all men were in astonishment; every day a tree is produced

31

from the dry earth, ... and no man wonders. ... Five thousand men were filled with five loaves; ... every day the grains of seed that are sown are multiplied in a fullness of ears, and no man wonders. All ... wondered to see water once turned into wine. Every day the earth's moisture, being drawn into the root of the vine, is turned by the grape into wine, and no man wonders. Full of wonder then are all the things which men never think to wonder at, because ... they are by habit become dull to the consideration of them.[7]

Holiness cannot be confined

WENDELL BERRY

I don't think it is enough appreciated how much an outdoor book the Bible is. It is a hypaethral book, such as Thoreau talked about—a book open to the sky. It is best read and understood outdoors, and the farther outdoors the better. Or that has been my experience of it. Passages that within walls seem improbable or incredible, outdoors seem merely natural. That is because outdoors we are confronted everywhere with wonders; we see that the miraculous is not extraordinary, but the common mode of existence. It is our daily bread. Whoever really has considered the lilies of the field or the birds of the air, and pondered the improbability of their existence in this warm world within the cold and empty stellar distances, will hardly balk at the fuming of water into wine—which

32

was, after all, a very small miracle. We forget the greater and still continuing miracle by which water (with soil and sunlight) is fumed into grapes.

What the Bible might mean, or how it could mean anything, in a closed, air-conditioned building, I do not know. I know that holiness cannot be confined. When you think you have captured it, it has already escaped; only its poor, pale ashes are left. It is after this foolish capture and the inevitable escape that you get translations of the Bible that read like a newspaper. Holiness is everywhere in Creation, it is as common as raindrops and leaves and blades of grass, but it does not sound like a newspaper.[8]

God saw how good it was

GENESIS 1:1–25

In the beginning when God created the heavens and the earth, the earth was a formless void and darkness covered the face of the deep, while a wind from God swept over the face of the waters. Then God said, "Let there be light"; and there was light. And God saw that the light was good; and God separated the light from the darkness. God called the light Day, and the darkness he called Night. And there was evening and there was morning, the first day.

And God said, "Let there be a dome in the midst of the waters, and let it separate the waters from the waters."

So God made the dome and separated the waters that were under the dome from the waters that were above the dome. And it was so. God called the dome Sky. And there was evening and there was morning, the second day.

And God said, "Let the waters under the sky be gathered together into one place, and let the dry land appear." And it was so. God called the dry land Earth, and the waters that were gathered together he called Seas. And God saw that it was good. Then God said, "Let the earth put forth vegetation: plants yielding seed, and fruit trees of every kind on earth that bear fruit with the seed in it." And it was so. The earth brought forth vegetation: plants yielding seed of every kind, and trees of every kind bearing fruit with the seed in it. And God saw that it was good. And there was evening and there was morning, the third day.

And God said, "Let there be lights in the dome of the sky to separate the day from the night; and let them be for signs and for seasons and for days and years, and let them be lights in the dome of the sky to give light upon the earth." And it was so. God made the two great lights—the greater light to rule the day and the lesser light to rule the night—and the stars. God set them in the dome of the sky to give light upon the earth, to rule over the day and over the night, and to separate the light from the darkness. And God saw that it was good. And there was evening and there was morning, the fourth day.

And God said, "Let the waters bring forth swarms of living creatures, and let birds fly above the earth across the dome of the sky." So God created the great sea monsters and every living creature that moves, of every kind, with which the waters swarm, and every winged bird of every kind. And God saw that it was good. God blessed them, saying, "Be fruitful and multiply and fill the waters in the seas, and let birds multiply on the earth." And there was evening and there was morning, the fifth day.

And God said, "Let the earth bring forth living creatures of every kind: cattle and creeping things and wild animals of the earth of every kind." And it was so. God made the wild animals of the earth of every kind, and the cattle of every kind, and everything that creeps upon the ground of every kind. And God saw that it was good.

How varied are your works

PSALM 104:1, 10–28

Bless the LORD, O my soul. O LORD my God, you are very great. . . .

You make springs gush forth in the valleys; they flow between the hills, giving drink to every wild animal; the wild asses quench their thirst.

By the streams the birds of the air have their habitation; they sing among the branches.

From your lofty abode you water the mountains; the earth is satisfied with the fruit of your work.

You cause the grass to grow for the cattle, and plants for people to use, to bring forth food from the earth, and wine to gladden the human heart, oil to make the face shine, and bread to strengthen the human heart.

The trees of the Lord are watered abundantly, the cedars of Lebanon that he planted.

In them the birds build their nests; the stork has its home in the fir trees.

The high mountains are for the wild goats; the rocks are a refuge for the coneys.

You have made the moon to mark the seasons; the sun knows its time for setting.

You make darkness, and it is night, when all the animals of the forest come creeping out.

The young lions roar for their prey, seeking their food from God.

When the sun rises, they withdraw and lie down in their dens.

People go out to their work and to their labor until the evening.

O Lord, how manifold are your works!

In wisdom you have made them all; the earth is full of your creatures.

Yonder is the sea, great and wide, creeping things innumerable are there, living things both small and great.

There go the ships, and Leviathan that you formed to sport in it.

These all look to you to give them their food in due season; when you give to them, they gather it up; when you open your hand, they are filled with good things.

I was there

PROVERBS 8:22–31

The LORD created me at the beginning of his work, the first of his acts of long ago.

Ages ago I was set up, at the first, before the beginning of the earth.

When there were no depths I was brought forth, when there were no springs abounding with water.

Before the mountains had been shaped, before the hills, I was brought forth—when he had not yet made earth and fields, or the world's first bits of soil.

When he established the heavens, I was there, when he drew a circle on the face of the deep, when he made firm the skies above, when he established the fountains of the deep, when he assigned to the sea its limit, so that the waters might not transgress his command, when he marked out the foundations of the earth, then I was beside him, like a master worker; and I was daily his delight, rejoicing before him always, rejoicing in his inhabited world and delighting in the human race.

We are astonished at tiny ants

AUGUSTINE OF HIPPO

What discourse can adequately describe the beauty and utility of creation, which the divine bounty has bestowed upon man to behold and consume? Consider the manifold and varied beauty of sky and earth and sea; the plenteousness of light and its wondrous quality, in the sun, moon and stars and in the shadows of the forests; the colour and fragrance of flowers; the diversity and multitude of the birds, with their songs and bright colours; the multiform species of living creatures of all kinds, even the smallest of which we behold with the greatest wonder—for we are more astonished at the feats of tiny ants and bees than we are at the immense bodies of the whales.

Consider also the grand spectacle of the sea, robing herself in different colours, like garments: sometimes green, and that in so many different shades; sometimes purple; sometimes blue. And what a delightful thing it is to behold the sea when stormy: a sight made all the more delightful to the onlooker by the pleasant thought that he is not a sailor being tossed and heaved about on it! Is there any limit to the abundant supply of food by which we are everywhere fortified against hunger? Or to the variety of flavours available to our fastidious tastes, lavishly distributed by the richness of nature, quite apart from the skill and labour of cooks? Consider also all the resources available to us for the preservation or recovery of health; the welcome alternation of day and night; the soothing coolness of breezes; all the material for our clothing furnished by plants and animals. Who could give a complete account of all these things?[9]

Your works are full of wonder

TRADITIONAL JEWISH PRAYER

How wonderful, O Lord, are the works of your hands! The heavens declare Your glory, the arch of sky displays Your handiwork. In Your love You have given us power to behold the beauty of Your world robed in all its splendor. The sun and the stars, the valleys and hills, the rivers and lakes all disclose Your presence. The roaring breakers of the sea tell of your awesome might, the beasts of the field and the birds of the air bespeak Your wondrous will. In Your goodness You have made us able to hear the music of the world. The voices of loved ones reveal to us that You are in our midst. A divine voice sings through all creation.

The glory of God fills all his works

SIRACH 43

The pride of the higher realms is the clear vault of the sky, as glorious to behold as the sight of the heavens.

The sun, when it appears, proclaims as it rises what a marvelous instrument it is, the work of the Most High. At noon it parches the land, and who can withstand its burning heat? A man tending a furnace works in burning heat, but three times as hot is the sun scorching the mountains; it breathes out fiery vapors, and its bright rays blind the eyes. Great is the Lord who made it; at his orders it hurries on its course.

It is the moon that marks the changing seasons, governing the times, their everlasting sign. From the moon comes the sign for festal days, a light that wanes when it completes its course. The new moon, as its name suggests, renews itself; how marvelous it is in this change, a beacon to the hosts on high, shining in the vault of the heavens!

The glory of the stars is the beauty of heaven, a glittering array in the heights of the Lord. On the orders of the Holy One they stand in their appointed places; they never relax in their watches. Look at the rainbow, and praise him who made it; it is exceedingly beautiful in its brightness. It encircles the sky with its glorious arc; the hands of the Most High have stretched it out.

By his command he sends the driving snow and speeds the lightnings of his judgment. Therefore the storehouses are opened, and the clouds fly out like birds. In his majesty he gives the clouds their strength, and the hailstones are broken in pieces. The voice of his thunder rebukes the earth; when he appears, the mountains shake. At his will the south wind blows; so do the storm from the north and the whirlwind.

He scatters the snow like birds flying down, and its descent is like locusts alighting. The eye is dazzled by the beauty of its whiteness, and the mind is amazed as it falls. He pours frost over the earth like salt, and icicles form like pointed thorns. The cold north wind blows, and ice freezes on the water; it settles on every pool of water, and the water puts it on like a breastplate. He consumes the mountains and burns up the wilderness, and withers the tender grass like fire. A mist quickly heals all things; the falling dew gives refreshment from the heat. By his plan he stilled the deep and planted islands in it. Those who sail the sea tell of its dangers, and we marvel at what we hear. In it are strange and marvelous creatures, all kinds of living things, and huge sea-monsters. Because of him each of his messengers succeeds, and by his word all things hold together. We could say more but could never say enough; let the final word be: "He is the all." Where can we find the strength to praise him? For he is greater than all his works. Awesome is the Lord and very great, and marvelous is his power. Glorify the Lord and exalt him as much as you can, for he surpasses even that. When you exalt him, summon all your strength, and do not grow weary, for you cannot praise him enough. Who has seen him and can describe him? Or who can extol him as he is? Many things greater than these lie hidden, for I have seen but few of his works. For the Lord has made all things, and to the godly he has given wisdom.

The whole universe

THOMAS AQUINAS

God brought things into being in order that the divine goodness might be communicated to creatures and be represented by them. And because the divine goodness could not be adequately represented by one creature alone, God produced many and diverse creatures, that what was wanting in one in the representation of divine goodness might be supplied by another. For goodness, which in God is simple and uniform, in creatures is manifest and divided. Thus the whole universe together participates in divine goodness more perfectly and represents it better than any single creature whatever.[10]

Enjoying the world

THOMAS TRAHERNE

You never enjoy the world aright . . .

Till you see how a sand exhibiteth the power and wisdom of God.

Till you can sing and rejoice and delight in God, as misers do in gold, and Kings in sceptres, you never enjoy the world.

Till your spirit filleth the whole world, and the stars are your jewels.

Till you are as familiar with the ways of God in all Ages as with your walk and table.

Till you are intimately acquainted with that shady nothing out of which the world was made. Till you love men so as to desire their happiness, with a thirst equal to the zeal of your own. Till you delight in God for being good to all, you never enjoy the world.

Till you more feel it than your private estate, and are more present in the hemisphere, considering the glories and the beauties there, than in your own house.

Till you remember how lately you were made, and how wonderful it was when you came into it and more rejoice in the palace of your glory, than if it had been made but today morning.

Yet further, you never enjoy the world aright, till you so love the beauty of enjoying it, that you are covetous and earnest to persuade others to enjoy it . . .

The world is a mirror of infinite beauty, yet no man sees it. It is a Temple of Majesty, yet no man regards it. It is a region of Light and Peace, did not men disquiet it. It is the Paradise of God. It is more to man since he is fallen than it was before. It is the place of Angels and the Gate of Heaven.[11]

43

The book of created nature

AUGUSTINE OF HIPPO

Others, in order to find God, will read a book. Well, as a matter of fact there is a certain great big book, the book of created nature. Look carefully at it top and bottom, observe it, read it. God did not make letters of ink for you to recognize him in; he set before your eyes all these things he had made. Why look for a louder voice? Heaven and earth cries out to you, "God made me." Observe heaven and earth in a religious spirit.[12]

Flowers

THÉRÈSE OF LISIEUX

He set before me the book of nature; I understood how all the flowers He has created are beautiful, how the splendor of the rose and the whiteness of the lily do not take away the perfume of the little violet or the delightful simplicity of the daisy. I understood that if all flowers wanted to be roses, nature would lose her springtime beauty, and the fields would no longer be decked out with little wild flowers. And so it is in the world of souls, Jesus' garden. . . . Perfection consists in doing His will, in being what He wills us to be.[13]

Their beauty is their confession

AUGUSTINE OF HIPPO

Knowing Him how? From the things He made. Question the beauty of the earth, question the beauty of the sea, question the beauty of the air, amply spread around everywhere, question the beauty of the sky, question the serried ranks of the stars, question the sun making the day glorious with its bright beams, question the moon tempering the darkness of the following night with its shining rays, question the animals that move in the waters, that amble about on dry land, that fly in the air . . . question all these things. They all answer you, "Here we are, look, we're beautiful."

Their beauty is their confession. Who made these beautiful changeable things, if not one who is beautiful and unchangeable?[14]

Your spirit is in all things

WISDOM 11:24–26

For you love all things that exist, and detest none of the things that you have made, for you would not have made anything if you had hated it. How would anything have endured if you had not willed it? Or how would anything not called forth by you have been preserved? You spare all things, for they are yours, O Lord, you who love the living.

Everything in God

JULIAN OF NORWICH

For God is all that is good, as I see it, and God has made all that is made, and God loves all that he has made . . . in man is God and God is in everything.

The fullness of joy is to see God in everything; for the same power, wisdom and love with which he made all things, our good Lord is continually leading all things to the same end and he himself shall bring this about.[15]

God made it, God loves it, God cares for it

JULIAN OF NORWICH

I saw that for us He is everything that we find good and comforting. He is our clothing, wrapping us for love, embracing and enclosing us for tender love, so that He can never leave us, being Himself everything that is good for us, as I understand it. In this vision He also showed me a little thing, the size of a hazelnut in the palm of my hand, and it was as round as a ball. I looked at it with my mind's eye and thought, "What can this be?" And the answer came to me, "It is all that is made." I wondered how it could last, for it was so small I thought it might suddenly have disappeared. And the answer in my mind was, "It lasts and will last for ever because God loves it; and everything exists in the same way by the love of God." In this little thing I saw three properties: the first is that God made it, the second is that God loves it, the third is that God cares for it.[16]

Three views from space

ASTRONAUT EDGAR MITCHELL

Thousands of miles away from here the Earth displays the incredible beauty of a marvelous blue and white jewel, floating in the vast dark sky . . . It fits in the palm of my hand.[17]

ASTRONAUT JAMES IRWIN

The Earth reminds me of a Christmas tree suspended against the black depths of the universe. The further away we go, the smaller it gets, until finally it is reduced to the most beautiful imaginable little ball. That living object, so beautiful and so warm, looks frail and delicate. Contemplating it changes a person, because you begin to appreciate God's creation and discover God's love.[18]

ASTRONAUT GENE CERNAN

When I was the last man to walk on the moon in December 1972, I stood in the blue darkness and looked in awe at the earth from the lunar surface. What I saw was almost too beautiful to grasp. There was too much logic, too much purpose—it was just too beautiful to have happened by accident. It doesn't matter how you choose to worship God . . . He has to exist to have created what I was privileged to see.[19]

And then I wander

WENDELL BERRY

And then I wander some more among the trees. There is a thought repeating itself in my mind: This is a great Work, this is a great Work. It occurs to me that my head has gone to talking religion, that it is going ahead more or less on its own, assenting to the Creation, finding it good, in the spirit of the first chapters of Genesis. For no matter the age or the hour, I am celebrating the morning of the seventh day, I assent to my mind's assent. It *is* a great Work. It is a *great* Work—begun in the beginning, carried on until now, to be carried on, not by such processes as men make or understand, but by "the kind of intelligence that enables grass seed to grow grass; the cherry stone to make cherries."[20]

2

Our Place in Creation

Encounters with nature are occasions for reflection. You can probably think of many examples in your own life. Some that come to mind for us are:

A former university student whose life is disordered goes winter camping in Minnesota with some friends. Living so close to freezing—to the edge of his own existence—forces him to evaluate his life. He begins to reorder things.

One of the authors recalls standing on the shore of a lake far from any town, gazing at the stars next to his son on a cloudless, moonless night. The young boy, in complete wonderment, says, "There has to be a God to make this."

On the other hand, there is nothing quite like being buzzed by a billion mosquitoes to cause us to think about the so-called dominance of humans over nature. Take a stroll through any campground on a summer night—look at the campers, sitting as one, slapping themselves silly and reeking of DEET before they flee into their tents.

Encounters with nature are invitations to reassess our lives and our place in the world. The selections in this chapter encourage us to reflect on nature and our relationship with it. Most people would agree with the point that one's view of the natural world influences how a person treats nature and that one's view of human nature influences one's view of human responsibility in and toward the natural world. We are invited to consider a "big question," namely, our view of what it means to be a person. This may seem overly philosophical, but in some ways you may have already addressed such questions, if you've thought about the meaning of life as you smacked another gnat.

The initial reading in this section is from Genesis, and it contains the famous phrase about man's "dominion" and man being made in God's image. It is a continuation of the creation story we read in the first portion of this book. The selection here begins with the "sixth" day of creation. This simple text is not without controversy. There have been times in history when Christians and Jews have used this text to justify exploitation of the earth's resources. In particular, the words *dominion* and *image* have been interpreted in ways that have been detrimental to the health of the planet. *Dominion*, for example, has been taken to mean something like *domination*, as if God created nature exclusively for the fulfillment of human desires.

More recently, some scholars have examined the original Hebrew translations. The word *image*, they suggest, comes from the same root as the word *viceroy*. A viceroy is a person appointed by a king to rule over a province. A viceroy has the responsibility to rule the province as the king would. Being created in God's image then suggests that humans are created to be God's responsible representatives on earth. The creation story portrays humans as having a preeminent place in creation as well as a determined responsibility for the well-being of creation. By the same token, *dominion* is better understood as stewardship than as domination. Humans are commissioned to take care of the earth, use it appropriately, keep it healthy and beautiful. The world, after all, belongs to God, not to us. It will endure long past our lives.

People living in highly industrialized areas often forget about their basic connection to nature. The Genesis story reminds us of our fundamental relationship to the "fish of the sea, the birds of the air and all living things that move on the earth." The culmination of creation is the Sabbath, where, we are told, God rests with the knowledge that all of creation is "very good." Thomas Merton (1915–1968), an internationally known spiritual figure, Trappist monk, poet, and best-selling author, pushes the question of value and valuing creation a bit further than does Genesis.

Merton lived most of his adult life in the community of the Abbey of Gethsemani in Kentucky. Churches are communities, of course, and also places where collective action can take place. More and more churches have taken leadership roles on environmental issues in recent years, many of them deriving inspiration from biblical texts. The writings of two Christian groups, the General Board of the American Baptist Churches and the Evangelical Environmental Network, are examples of the positions taken by such organizations on the relationship between humans and the environment.

Concern for the environment and conservationism are moral and indeed spiritual concerns. Pope John Paul II (1920–) was an avid hiker and skier in his youth. The pope expresses the sentiments of many Christians. His strong words call us to reflect on human, personal, and social responsibility. The Evangelical Lutheran Church reflects on the moral principle of "sustainability." These are good examples of appropriate Christian responses to nature. They proportionally weigh the tensions between the ideas that creation is God's handiwork and is in a sense "sacred"; that humanity flourishing is utterly dependent on creation; and that humans have selfishly spoiled the earth, using rivers, lakes, seas, and the air as if they were garbage cans or sewers.

It is not unusual for various religious groups to organize around political, moral, and social issues. Such meetings are often called by the churches themselves. In 1984, the United Nations Environment Programme began an initiative with many of the world's religions. It encouraged each religion to examine its teachings on the environment and to take time to learn what other religions teach. It called the event the "Environmental Sabbath" or "Earth Rest Day," and it is observed every June 3.

———•◦•———

Sometimes apart from churches, philosophers and theologians have long wrestled with our relationship to nature. They have offered four typical responses.[1] The first, and perhaps most popular, is to believe that the fundamental purpose of nature is to fulfill human needs. If one holds this belief, then he or she believes that we are allowed and indeed expected to use nature as we see fit. Nature has been given to us by God to fulfill our basic needs and desires. Creation serves a utility value for humans. Its "goodness" lies in the fact that it is good for us.

The second typical response, one preached by many religions for generations, is that we are stewards of the earth. We are responsible to God, our children, their children, and perhaps our ancestors. We are thus to use creation wisely to fulfill our needs and desires. We are God's representatives on earth. There are appropriate and inappropriate uses of creation. We should not exhaust it or despoil it.

The third position, unlike the first and second views, rejects the idea that humans are "superior to" or "better than" the rest of creation. It holds that there is a fundamental equality or parity within nature. This response is perhaps the most radical one. People who hold this position would argue that animals have as much right to their existence as do humans. Animals can make moral claims on people. If the first two positions separate humans from nature, the third rejects humanity's claim of moral dominance. We are but one species among many. Thus to speak of "managing" nature is to put humans in an unwarranted controlling position.

The fourth position mediates between the second and third responses. It holds onto the view expressed in the "responsible representative" position that humans have a unique position of power within nature and must use it responsibly. At the same time, influenced by the third position, it notes that humans are indeed a part of the interdependent web of creation. We are participants in nature with all of creation. Humans are connected to the patterns and processes of nature.

In summary the four positions are: One, creation is for humans. Two, humans are to be stewards of creation. Three, humans, part of creation, hold a moral equivalence with creation. Four, humans are to be responsible for creation while at the same time recognizing they are interdependent within creation. We, the authors of this book, lean toward the last position. Where do you stand?

The Links between Humans and Creation

Humans' connections to creation as well as the link we have to God through creation have been a popular area of thought. In folklore, sometimes speeches and texts are attributed to well-known people, but further investigation finds that the words are actually penned by others. Two examples are the words of Christian saints Patrick and Francis, and a third is by the Native American leader Chief Seattle. Each text appeared some time after the author's death. A disciple or scholar of the deceased man in his spirit and tradition wrote each passage, sometimes crediting the mentor.

55

Patrick (390–460) knew about hardship and the travails of nature. At the age of sixteen, he was kidnapped by Irish raiders from his home in Britain. He was brought to Ireland and forced into the life of a shepherd on a desolate mountain. After six years of slavery he escaped and returned home. Years later he came back to Ireland as a Christian missionary. To this day, he is remembered as the person who brought Christianity to Ireland. A remarkable element of his story is that he returned to Ireland, not in anger or out of revenge, but in faith. This faith developed and matured during his long years in exile on the lonely mountain. His famous Breastplate prayer is indicative of Patrick's spirituality and the spirituality of his followers for years to come. Note his prayer for protection, his confidence in nature, and his sense of the presence of Christ.

There is a famous story of a conversation Patrick had with daughters of a pagan king. They asked him questions about his God. "Where does your god live? Is your god beautiful?" Patrick answered, again with a confidence in nature and a solid sense of the presence of God, "Our God is the God of all things, the God of heaven and earth and sea and river, the God of sun and moon and all the stars, the God of high mountains and lowly valleys; the God over heaven and in heaven and under heaven. He has a dwelling both in heaven and earth and seas and all that dwell within them. He inspires all things, he gives life to all things; he surpasses all things. Our God kindles the light of the sun and the light of the moon. He made springs in arid land and dry islands in the sea, and stars he appointed to minister to the greater lights."[2] Tradition has it that at this point Patrick reached down to pull a shamrock, a three-leaf clover, out of the ground to explain and symbolize the Trinity to the women. Patrick knew that we could see something about God by reflecting on God's creation.

———•••———

The person in Christian history most often associated with nature, the environment, gardens, and animals is Francis of Assisi (1182–1226). Francis, like Augustine before him, led a life of pleasure as a young man. Through a series of events he turned his life around. One of the most frequently told stories of his life occurred not long after he became serious about his faith. While he prayed in a dilapidated church he heard a voice. "Francis," it said, "repair my church, which has fallen into disrepair." Francis followed these words with great gusto and immediately set out to repair the building (using his father's money!). Later he came to understand the words in a spiritual sense. He was to help renew the people of God.

The famous prayer uses words of the family to describe natural phenomena. Francis calls the sun our brother and the moon our sister. This is surprising language, because we do not tend to think of ourselves as being biologically related to things such as water, wind, fire, and earth—the ancient elements. These are the things thought in old times to form the material substance of physical reality. They are, says Francis, our family. We see God's ways in their existence.

One of the most quoted statements attributed to a Native American is Chief Seattle's address on nature and the nature of humans. Sometime between 1853 and 1855, Seattle gave a speech in what is now the state of Washington. Seattle (1786–1866), chief of the Suquamish tribe, had in his audience one Dr. Henry Smith, who, many years later—in October 1887—published an embellished copy of the oration in the Seattle *Sunday Star* newspaper. A later, entirely fictionalized version, written in the early 1970s by Ted Perry for a documentary film made for the Southern Baptist Convention, remains today the most widely circulated text of Seattle's words. This reading is not explicitly Christian, but note how the author draws Christian themes into the address.

Attitudes toward Creation

A text credited to the prophet Isaiah in the Old Testament some 2,800 years ago is surprisingly, indeed shockingly, relevant. Although popular thinking might have pollution as a post–Industrial Age problem, this reading from Isaiah tells us that the idea of pollution is as ancient as the Hebrew scriptures. Pollution, the desecration of God's earth (breaking the covenant), as described by Isaiah, is the result of human behavior.

The "everlasting covenant" referred to here is from Genesis 9, the time of the great flood, when Noah, in association with every living creation, becomes a partner in a covenant with God. Covenants are solemn agreements laying out rights and responsibilities for the parties involved. Isaiah states that the people have broken the covenant, thus threatening the natural order. When the covenant is broken, the earth dries up, becoming withered, barren, and polluted.

Why is the earth polluted? One biblically based answer says that it is because of a lack of responsible stewardship. Indeed one wonders today if there is an unpolluted place on earth. Tall peaks like Mt. Everest are littered with the trash of hundreds of climbers; acid rain falls on the great, remote northern forests; waters everywhere flow thick with sludge. Campsites in seldom-used parks and along forgotten trails contain the litter of travelers gone by. In wilderness settings, there are many aspects of responsibility. We ought not to forget that we must be accountable for our actions. As the saying goes, we ought to "leave no trace" when we hike or fish. Responsibility has other ramifications. It also means being responsive to the needs and wishes of those with whom you are traveling. Responsible stewards, moreover, continue their concern for the well-being of the wilderness long after they have returned home.

———•◦•———

Fyodor Dostoyevsky's *The Brothers Karamazov,* first published in 1879, is as dramatic in its way as Isaiah. *The Brothers Karamazov* remains a classic text. The book contains several unforgettable characters, including Father Zosima. The priest, in contrast to some rather vile figures in the book, is a sage and generous person. Dostoyevsky (1821–1881) presents Zosima as a man with keen insight into the human condition. Because the scene where this text takes place is Zosima's deathbed, it is empowered with a sense of urgency.

———•◦•———

The word *sublime* is not often used in everyday discourse. The word is indeed a bit hard to define. *Sublime* refers to something awe-inspiring, beautiful, and impressive. A sublime event or thing has high moral and/or spiritual worth. It lifts us. It is, in a word, heavenly. A sense of the sublime, a sense of the sacred, can be missing in our highly developed, technological society. Pierre Teilhard de Chardin calls us to sense the sublime. Teilhard (1881–1955) was a French priest, paleontologist, biologist, and philosopher. His life's work was to integrate religious experience with natural science. This is not an easy task. Science promises to give us explanations for nearly all things. Technology feeds our needs and creates our needs. Our entertainment and communication devices give us instant messages, instant feedback, and constantly changing images. At times we all need to leave this environment and touch a simpler life. If an earlier time was suspicious of material reality in deference to things spiritual, our time might be said to see material reality merely for its usefulness. In our constant task of seeking of pleasure, we ignore the spiritual reality that surrounds us. Teilhard's words remind us of the spiritual effort involved in "making our way" through the exertion of our existence. He uses the image of ascent, much like the mountain climber, lifting our spirits, lifting our souls, in contrast to the tendency we have to fall into selfishness.

When you prepare yourself for a canoe trip or walk in the park, do not forget to "pack" a disposition of openness to the beauty of the calm of a lake stretched out before you or the trees, birds, and flowers you will pass on your hike. Your disposition, not your course, will determine whether or not you are heading in a good direction.

Owning the Earth

The concept of "owning" a part of the earth invites all sorts of interesting moral and religious questions. The earth is God's. We do not ultimately own the earth or any part of the earth. "Ownership" is a human, not a divine, invention. Yet we do own things. Human society would be very different, and perhaps unlivable, if there were no ownership of things. "Ownership" serves many social goods; even in families, where many things are held in common, moms and dads and kids have their "own" things. Common wisdom suggests that homeowners tend to take better care of their homes than do renters. On the other hand, as every homeowner knows, just because we own something does not mean we can do anything we want with it.

A number of religious and cultural traditions address this issue. Ambrose (339–397), an important Christian leader of his day, writes about ownership and the moral meaning of ownership. *The Analects of Confucius* (551–479 BCE) contains the thoughts of the ancient Chinese philosopher—who is not commonly thought of as an environmentalist, or even religious, but certainly he had a lot to say on the proper way (*dao*) to live a life. Eastern philosophers often comment on the meaning of possessions. So does the Talmud, which was completed in the fifth century CE and is a record of the oral commentary and tradition of rabbinical teaching on the first five books of the Bible, the Torah.

We end these remarks with the words of a contemporary theologian Steven Bouma-Prediger. He writes, "Authentic Christian faith requires ecological obedience.

To care for the earth is integral to Christian faith ... if we do not properly understand our home planet, we will not properly understand the nature and character of the God we worship and claim to serve. Therefore, nothing less than our understanding of God is at stake."[3]

In our image

GENESIS 1:26–31

Then God said, "Let us make humankind in our image, according to our likeness; and let them have dominion over the fish of the sea, and over the birds of the air, and over the cattle, and over all the wild animals of the earth, and over every creeping thing that creeps upon the earth."

So God created humankind in his image, in the image of God he created them; male and female he created them.

God blessed them, and God said to them, "Be fruitful and multiply, and fill the earth and subdue it; and have dominion over the fish of the sea and over the birds of the air and over every living thing that moves upon the earth." God said, "See, I have given you every plant yielding seed that is upon the face of all the earth, and every tree with seed in its fruit; you shall have them for food. And to every beast of the earth, and to every bird of the air, and to everything that creeps on the earth, everything that has the breath of life, I have given every green plant

63

for food." And it was so. God saw everything that he had made, and indeed, it was very good. And there was evening and there was morning, the sixth day.

The fragility of humans

PSALM 8:1–9

O Lord, our Sovereign, how majestic is your name in all the earth! You have set your glory above the heavens.

Out of the mouths of babes and infants you have founded a bulwark because of your foes, to silence the enemy and the avenger.

When I look at your heavens, the work of your fingers, the moon and the stars that you have established; what are human beings that you are mindful of them, mortals that you care for them?

Yet you have made them a little lower than God, and crowned them with glory and honor.

You have given them dominion over the works of your hands; you have put all things under their feet, all sheep and oxen, and also the beasts of the field, the birds of the air, and the fish of the sea, whatever passes along the paths of the seas.

O Lord, our Sovereign, how majestic is your name in all the earth!

Catching glimpses of God

THOMAS MERTON

What is serious to men is often very trivial in the sight of God. What in God might appear to us as "play" is perhaps what God takes the most seriously. At any rate the Lord plays in the garden of creation, and if we could let go of our own obsession with what we think is the meaning of it all, we might be able to hear God's call and follow in the mysterious, cosmic dance. We do not have to go very far to catch echoes of that game, and of that dancing. When we are alone on a starlit night; when by chance we see the migrating birds in autumn descending on a grove of junipers to rest and eat; when we see children in a moment when they are really children; when we know love in our own hearts; or when, like the Japanese poet Basho, we hear an old frog land in a quiet pond with a solitary splash—at such times the awakening, the turning inside out of all values, the "newness," the emptiness and the purity of vision that make themselves evident, provide a glimpse of the cosmic dance.[4]

Creation and the covenant of caring

GENERAL BOARD OF THE AMERICAN BAPTIST CHURCHES

The earth belongs to God, as affirmed in Psalm 24:1. We are caretakers or stewards. Thus we are each related to God as one appointed to take care of someone else's possessions entrusted to us—our life, our home, the earth. The vast resources of the earth can provide for all its inhabitants, or they can be greedily swallowed up or poisoned by a few without regard for the impact of their actions.

The best understanding of the Biblical attitude of humanity's relationship with the Creation can be gained by a study of the Greek words which are the foundation of the New Testament. The word "stewardship" comes from the Greek words for house and management. The Greek word which is commonly translated "stewardship" is the root word for economics and ecology. The literal translation of steward is manager of the household. As such, we are all called to be managers of God's household, the earth and all that is in it.

Our responsibility as stewards is one of the most basic relationships we have with God. It implies a great degree of caring for God's creation and all God's creatures. The right relationship is embodied in the everlasting covenant to which Isaiah refers. There can be no justice without right relationships of creatures with one another and with all of creation. Eco-justice is the vision of the garden in Genesis—the realm and the reality of right relationship.[5]

On the care of creation

EVANGELICAL ENVIRONMENTAL NETWORK

As followers of Jesus Christ, committed to the full authority of the Scriptures, and aware of the ways we have degraded creation, we believe that biblical faith is essential to the solution of our ecological problems.... God calls us to confess and repent of attitudes which devalue creation, and which twist or ignore biblical revelation to support our misuse of it. Forgetting that "the earth is the Lord's," we have often simply used creation and forgotten our responsibility to care for it.... Our God-given, stewardly talents have often been warped from their intended purpose: that we know, name, keep and delight in God's creatures; that we nourish civilization in love, creativity and obedience to God; and that we offer creation and civilization back in praise to the Creator. We have ignored our creaturely limits and have used the earth with greed, rather than care.... The earthly result of human sin has been a perverted stewardship, a patchwork of garden and wasteland in which the waste is increasing. "There is no faithfulness, no love, no acknowledgment of God in the land.... Because of this the land mourns, and all who live in it waste away" (Hosea 4:1, 3). Thus, one consequence of our misuse of the earth is an unjust denial of God's created bounty to other human beings, both now and in the future.[6]

67

A moral commitment

POPE JOHN PAUL II

It is well known how urgent it is to spread awareness that the resources of our planet must be respected. All are involved here because the world that we inhabit reveals ever more clearly its intrinsic unity, such that the problems of conservation of its patrimony concern peoples without distinction.

The conservation and development of woods, in whatever zone, are fundamental for the maintenance and the recomposition of the natural balances, which are indispensable for life. This must be affirmed all the more today as we become aware how urgent it is to change decisively the tendency in all that leads to a disturbing form of pollution. Each single person is obliged to avoid initiatives and actions that could damage the purity of the environment. Since trees and plant life, as a whole, have an indispensable function with regard to the balance of nature, so necessary to life in all its stages, it is a matter of ever-greater importance for mankind that they be protected and respected.

For the Christian there is a moral commitment to care for the earth so that it may produce fruit and become a dwelling of the universal human family.[7]

Sustainability

EVANGELICAL LUTHERAN CHURCH IN AMERICA

The principle of sustainability means providing an acceptable quality of life for present generations without compromising that of future generations.

Protection of species and their habitats, preservation of clean land and water, reduction of wastes, care of the land—these are priorities. But production of basic goods and services, equitable distribution, accessible markets, stabilization of population, quality education, full employment—these are priorities as well.

We recognize the obstacles to sustainability. Neither economic growth that ignores environmental cost nor conservation of nature that ignores human cost is sustainable. Both will result in injustice and, eventually, environmental degradation. We know that a healthy economy can exist only within a healthy environment, but that it is difficult to promote both in our decisions.

The principle of sustainability summons our church, in its global work with poor people, to pursue sustainable development strategies. It summons our church to support U.S. farmers who are turning to sustainable methods, and to encourage industries to produce sustainably. It summons each of us, in every aspect of our lives, to behave in ways that are consistent with the long-term sustainability of our planet.

We pray, therefore, for the creativity and dedication to live more gently with the earth.[8]

Environmental Sabbath I

UNITED NATIONS ENVIRONMENT PROGRAMME

We have forgotten who we are. We have alienated ourselves from the unfolding of the cosmos. We have become estranged from the movements of the earth. We have turned our backs on the cycles of life.

We have forgotten who we are. We have sought only our own security. We have exploited simply for our own ends. We have distorted our knowledge. We have abused our power.

We have forgotten who we are. Now the land is barren. And the waters are poisoned. And the air is polluted.

We have forgotten who we are. Now the forests are dying. And the creatures are disappearing. And humans are despairing.

We have forgotten who we are. We ask forgiveness. We ask for the gift of remembering. We ask for the strength to change.

We join with the earth and with each other. To bring new life to the land. To restore the waters. To refresh the air.

We join with the earth and with each other. To renew the forests. To care for the plants. To protect the creatures.

We join with the earth and with each other. To celebrate the seas. To rejoice in the sunlight. To sing the song of the stars.

We join with the earth and with each other. To recall our destiny. To renew our spirits. To reinvigorate our bodies.

We join with the earth and with each other. To recreate the human community. To promote justice and peace. To remember our children.

We join with the earth and with each other. We join together as many and diverse expressions of one loving mystery: for the healing of the earth and the renewal of all life.

We rejoice in all life! We live in all things. All things live in us. We rejoice in all life! We live by the sun. We move with the stars. We rejoice in all life! We eat from the earth. We drink from the rain. We breathe the air. We rejoice in all life! We share with the creatures. We have strength through their gifts. We rejoice in all life! We depend on the forests. We have knowledge through their secrets. We rejoice in all life! We have the privilege of seeing and understanding. We have the responsibility of caring. We have the joy of celebrating. We rejoice in all life! We are full of the grace of creation. We are graceful. We are grateful. We rejoice in all life![9]

Environmental Sabbath II

UNITED NATIONS ENVIRONMENT PROGRAMME

O Great Spirit, Whose breath gives life to the world and whose voice is heard in the soft breeze, we need your strength and wisdom. May we walk in Beauty. May our eyes ever behold the red and purple sunset. Make us wise so that we may understand what you have taught us. Help us learn the lessons you have hidden in every leaf and rock. Make us always ready to come to you with clean hands and straight eyes, so when life fades, as the fading sunset, our spirits may come to you without shame.[10]

The Breastplate of St. Patrick

PATRICK OF IRELAND

I awake today in power's strength, invoking the Trinity, believing in threeness, confessing the oneness, of Creation's Creator . . .

I awake today in Heaven's might and in the brightness of the Sun, in Moon's radiance and in glory of Fire, in Lightning quickness and in the swiftness of the Wind, in the Sea's depth and in the stability of the Earth.

I awake today with the power of God to guide me, the strength of God to sustain me, the wisdom of God to teach me, God's eye to look ahead of me, God's ear to hear me, God's word to speak to me, God's hand to protect me, God's way before me, God's shield to shelter me, God's host to deliver me from the snares of devils, evil temptations, nature's failings, all who wish to harm me, far or near, alone and in a crowd.

As I awake today may Christ today protect me against poison and burning, drowning and wounding, so that I may have abundant reward; Christ with me, Christ before me, Christ behind me; Christ within me, Christ beneath me, Christ above me; Christ to the right of me; Christ to the left of me; Christ in my lying, Christ in my sitting, Christ in my rising; Christ in the hearts of all who think of me, Christ on the tongues of all who speak to me, Christ in the eyes of all who see me, Christ in the ears of all who hear me.

I awake today in power's strength, invoking the Trinity, believing in threeness, confessing the oneness, of Creation's Creator.[11]

Canticle of the sun

St. Francis of Assisi

O most High, almighty, good Lord God, to you belong praise, glory, honor, and all blessing!

Praised be my Lord God with all creatures; and especially our brother the sun, which brings us the day and the light; fair is he, and shining with a very great splendor:

O Lord, he signifies you to us!

Praised be my Lord for our sister the moon, and for the stars, which God has set clear and lovely in heaven.

Praised be my Lord for our brother the wind, and for air and cloud, calms and all weather, by which you uphold in life all creatures.

Praised be my Lord for our sister water, which is very serviceable to us, and humble, and precious, and clean.

Praised be my Lord for brother fire, through which you give us light in the darkness; and he is bright, and pleasant, and very mighty, and strong.

Praised be my Lord for our mother the Earth, which sustains us and keeps us, and yields diverse fruits, and flowers of many colors, and grass.

Praised be my Lord for all those who pardon one another for God's love's sake, and who endure weakness and tribulation; blessed are they who peaceably shall endure, for you, O most High, shall give them a crown!

Praised be my Lord for our sister, the death of the body, from which no one escapes. Woe to him who died in mortal sin!

Blessed are they who are found walking by your most holy will, for the second death shall have no power to do them harm.

Praise you, and bless you the Lord, and give thanks to God, and serve God with great humility.[12]

Chief Seattle's address

TED PERRY

How can you buy or sell the sky? The land? The idea is strange to us. If we do not own the freshness of the air and the sparkle of the water, how can you buy them?

Every part of the earth is sacred to my people. Every shining pine needle, every sandy shore, every mist in the dark woods, every meadow, every humming insect. All are holy in the memory and experience of my people.

We know the sap which courses through the trees as we know the blood that courses through our veins. We are part of the earth and it is part of us. The perfumed flowers are our sisters. The bear, the deer, the great eagle, these are our brothers. The rocky crests, the dew in the meadow, the body heat of the pony, and man all belong to the same family.

The shining water that moves in the streams and rivers is not just water, but the blood of our ancestors. If we sell you our land, you must remember that it is sacred. Each glossy reflection in the clear waters of the lakes tells of events and memories in the life of my people. The water's murmur is the voice of my father's father.

The rivers are our brothers. They quench our thirst. They carry our canoes and feed our children. So you must give the rivers the kindness that you would give any brother.

If we sell you our land, remember that the air is precious to us, that the air shares its spirit with all the life that it supports. The wind that gave our grandfather his first breath also received his last sigh. The wind also gives our children the spirit of life. So if we sell our land, you must keep it apart and sacred, as a place where man can go to taste the wind that is sweetened by the meadow flowers.

Will you teach your children what we have taught our children? That the earth is our mother? What befalls the earth befalls all the sons of the earth.

This we know: The earth does not belong to humans; humans belong to the earth. All things are connected like the blood that unites us all. Humans did not weave the web of life, they are merely a strand in it. Whatever humans do to the web, they do to themselves.

One thing we know: our God is also your God. The earth is precious to God and to harm the earth is to heap contempt on its creator.[13]

The earth is polluted

ISAIAH 24:4–5

The earth dries up and withers, the world languishes and withers; the heavens languish together with the earth. The earth lies polluted under its inhabitants; for they have transgressed laws, violated the statutes, broken the everlasting covenant.

Father Zosima

FYODOR DOSTOYEVSKY

Love all God's creation, the whole and every grain of
sand in it. Love every leaf, every ray of God's light. Love
the animals, love the plants, love everything. If you love
everything, you will perceive the divine mystery in things.
Once you perceive it, you will begin to comprehend it
better every day. Any of you will come at last to love
the whole world with an all-embracing love. Love the
animals: God has given them the rudiments of thought
and joy untroubled. Do not trouble it, don't harass them,
don't deprive them of their happiness, don't work against
God's intent. Man, do not pride yourself on superiority
to the animals; they are without sin, and you, with your
greatness, defile the earth. . . . When you are left alone,
pray. Love to throw yourself on the earth and kiss it. Kiss
the earth and love it with an unceasing, consuming love.
Love all men, love everything.[14]

There is only a good direction and a bad direction

PIERRE TEILHARD DE CHARDIN

All around us, to right and left, in front and behind,
above and below, we have only to go a little beyond the
frontier of sensible appearances in order to see the divine
welling up and showing through. But it is not only close
to us, in front of us, that the divine presence has revealed

itself. It has sprung up universally, and we find ourselves so surrounded and transfixed by it, that there is no room left to fall down and adore it, even within ourselves. By means of all created things, without exception, the divine assails us, penetrates us and molds us. We imagined it as distant and inaccessible, whereas in fact we live steeped in its burning layers. . . .

Material creation no longer stretches between man and God like a fog or a barrier. It develops like an elevating, enriching ambience; and it is important not to try to escape from this or release oneself from it, but to accept its reality and make our way through it. Rightly speaking, there are no sacred or profane things, no pure or impure: there is only a good direction and a bad direction—the direction of ascent, of amplifying unity, of greatest spiritual effort; and the direction of descent, of constricting egoism, of materializing enjoyment.[15]

The earth belongs to all—not just to the rich

St. Ambrose

You rich, how far will you push your frenzied greed? Are you alone to dwell on the earth? Why do you cast out men who are fellow-creatures and claim all creation as your own? Earth at its beginning was for all in common, it was meant for rich and poor alike; what right have you to monopolize the soil? . . . The world was created for all in general, yet a handful of the rich endeavor to make it their own preserve. . . . Indeed what is common to all and has been given to all to make use of, you have usurped for yourself alone. The earth belongs to all, and not only to the rich.[16]

The way

CONFUCIUS BOOK 4.5

The Master said, "Wealth and honor are what people want, but if they are the consequence of deviating from the way [*dao*], I would have no part in them. Poverty and disgrace are what people deplore, but if they are the consequence of staying on the way, I would not avoid them. Wherein do the exemplary persons who would abandon their authoritative conduct warrant that name? Exemplary persons do not take leave of their authoritative conduct even for the space of a meal. When they are troubled, they certainly turn to it, as they do in facing difficulties."[17]

Water: humble yet great

LAO TZU, TAO TE CHING 8

The highest good is like that of water. The goodness of water is that it benefits the ten thousand creatures; yet itself does not scramble, but is content with the places that all men disdain. It is this that makes water so near to the Way.[18]

A fight over ownership

THE TALMUD

Two men were fighting over a piece of land. Each claimed ownership and bolstered his claim with apparent proof. To resolve their differences, they agreed to put the case before the rabbi. The rabbi listened but could not come to a decision because both seemed to be right. Finally he said, "Since I cannot decide to whom this land belongs, let us ask the land." He put his ear to the ground, and after a moment straightened up. "Gentlemen, the land says that it belongs to neither of you—but that you belong to it."

3

That Special Spot

Much of the writing about spirituality and nature concerns itself with the meaning of a special place. And the granddaddy of all special spots for many Christians is heaven.

Actually, heaven has been a topic of considerable debate among Christians through the ages. There seem to be two general strands of thought on this matter: the first is that heaven is a particular state of "being." According to this view, heaven refers to the fulfillment of human existence in God. It is the state of perfect happiness or union with Christ when we have direct intuitive knowledge of God.

The second sense of heaven is that it is a divine place. Heaven is where God lives. It is our spiritual home, a place we go after death. It is this second view that has captured more of the imagination of Christians, who often tend to think of heaven as a beautiful, blissful place. It is a part of our cultural imagination; witness its use in popular phrases as such: *Good heavens! Heaven help us. She is heaven-sent.* And so on. Outdoors, it is not unusual for Christians to experience a place, most frequently a place in the wilderness, along a river or sea, and think that heaven must be, in some greater way, like that spot. How often have we heard another phrase: "a little heaven on earth"? We sometimes use terms like *utopia* and *Shangri-La* (from the novel *Lost Horizon*, by James Hilton) to mean an imaginary paradise on earth. Yet it is not just the beauty that captures our attention in such places. It is the feeling we get when we are there. In this way heaven is not just a "place." It is a way of "being."

This chapter explores the notion of special or sacred places: "heavens on earth." It has two parts: the first looks at the general idea of such a place, and the second examines geographical areas like rivers, seas, and mountains that seem to invite us to stop and consider the divine presence in our lives.[1]

Thin Places

Have you ever had the sense that you were in a special or sacred place? Have you ever felt that a particular place caused a sense of awe or wonder in your heart? Did that spot make you feel closer to God or connected to something much larger than yourself and your life? Perhaps that experience was not as dramatic as Moses's encounter with God on Mount Horeb. In the Exodus narrative God commands Moses to take off his sandals, for he is on "holy ground" (Exod. 3:4). Some spiritual writers refer to such spots as "thin places." This idea, while not rejecting the notion that God is transcendent being and creator of all, highlights the immanence or presence of God in human experience. The concept of a "thin place" or a "thin time" suggests that in certain places or at times the veil separating this world from the spiritual realm may be permeable or at least translucent. In the words of Gerard Manley Hopkins, "the world is charged with the grandeur of God."[2]

The Bible begins with a story about such a place, the Garden of Eden. *Eden* is the name of a region in southern Mesopotamia; the term is derived from the Sumerian word *eden,* meaning "fertile plain." A similar-sounding word means "delight" in Hebrew and Greek. Just the mention of the Garden of Eden evokes images of pleasure, peacefulness, and fulfillment. Indeed, it is often referred to as paradise or the Garden of Paradise.

When Eden is mentioned elsewhere in the Bible (Isa. 51:3, Ezra 28:13, Joel 2:3) images of vibrancy, fertility, and giant trees are included. If the Garden of Eden is the first special spot in salvation history, heaven is the final special spot. It is little wonder that in the Christian imagination, heaven and Eden are often blurred.

Jesus must have had a special spot or two. The New Testament suggests that on several occasions Jesus went off by himself to pray. Others took him up on the idea; this theme is found throughout the Christian tradition. A selection from the British monk Alcuin (735?–804) captures what one might find as one leaves one's cell, or in contemporary context, as one leaves one's cabin. Alcuin was a deacon, scholar, and teacher of science and math. Known as Charlemagne's "Minister of Culture," he encouraged the study of ancient texts and is said to have invented cursive writing, the form of writing we use daily that allows us to write faster by tying the letters of a word together.

Bernard of Clairvaux (1090–1153) was a bold, intelligent, and deeply religious man who was widely recognized as a leader in twelfth-century Europe. He was a man of interesting contradictions. Bernard was first and foremost a monk who lived an austere life of prayer. He was also a writer and preacher whose books on love for God and commentaries on the Song of Songs are still read and admired today. Bernard was at the same time deeply involved in the politics of his day. He argued with the emperor, was involved in a dispute over the papacy, and preached the Second Crusade.

The selection in this chapter is from Bernard's essay "Description of the Position and Site of the Abbey of Clairvaux." He begins the essay, "If you wish to know the site of Clairvaux, these lines will describe it for you as if in a mirror." His words are rich and generous as he describes the two mountains and valley where his abbey sits. In a striking passage, he speaks about how the sick are comforted as they sit beneath trees on the mountain. "Under their leafy screen the sun's rays are softened, and their sufferings are soothed as they breathe the air fragrant with the scent of hay. The pleasant green of the trees and of the turf rests their eyes, and the fruit which hangs before them promises them delight when ripened."[3] We sense that he has been in "that spot" often. The flowers, their fragrance, their beauty are a call to prayer for him.

This section includes selections from several contemporary authors, including Sigurd Olson (1899–1982). A writer, educator, wilderness guide, and conservationist, Olson was born in Chicago and raised in northern Wisconsin. He lived most of his adult life in Ely, Minnesota, near the wilderness where he felt most at home. His résumé of conservation work is long and his list of recognitions impressive. That the Sierra Club, the Wilderness Society, the National Wildlife Federation, and the Izaak Walton League all presented him with their highest awards indicates the significance of his work. Olson published nine books on nature, and many more articles and essays, and was awarded the highest honor in nature writing, the Burroughs Medal.

Olson believed that the wilderness provided people the opportunity for significant spiritual experiences. He thought that the wilderness allowed people to experience their primitive nature and that through this they could come to know basic spiritual values. In 1965 he wrote, "I have discovered in a lifetime of traveling in primitive regions, a lifetime of seeing people living in the wilderness and using it, that there is a hard core of wilderness need in everyone, a core that makes its spiritual values a basic human necessity. There is no hiding it.... Unless we can preserve places where the endless spiritual needs of man can be fulfilled and nourished, we will destroy our culture and ourselves."[4] In his many years as a canoe guide in what became known as the Boundary Waters Canoe Area Wilderness, Olson witnessed how city folk, normally governed by watches and schedules, transform as their bodies begin to conform to the rhythms of nature.[5]

———•◦•———

Edward Abbey (1927–1989) spent the summers of 1956 and 1957 as a park ranger in Arches National Park in Utah. He kept a journal—four volumes of notes—that was edited and published in 1968 as *Desert Solitaire* after he had spent years of knocking around the country in a series of odd jobs. After the first run of 10,000, *Desert Solitaire* went quietly out of print; not until 1975 and the success of his controversial novel *The Monkey Wrench Gang* was Abbey able to quit his job as a bus driver on an Indian reservation and retire to life as an author; *Desert Solitaire* was reissued. Abbey was not a religious man, and his books, at least on their surface, do not contain spiritual themes, yet he commonly quotes from a wide range of sources, including scripture. One special spot for him was the Arches, and when surveyors came in with plans to build more roads, he did not return to his job as a summer ranger. To those who fought for wilderness preservation and lost, he said, "Don't get discouraged, comrades—Christ failed too."[6]

———•◦•———

Annie Dillard (1945–) is the author of several books, including the Pulitzer Prize-winning *Pilgrim at Tinker*

Creek. The intersection of human, divine, and nature is a dominant theme in her writing. Her "special spot" is Tinker Creek in the Blue Ridge Mountains of Virginia, Roanoke Valley. James Silas Rogers (1952–), a contemporary Minnesota writer with an interest in pilgrimage and sacred geography, writes about a formative experience he had in his early twenties while traveling in County Mayo, Ireland. Camping along Clew Bay, he happened upon a place where he experienced "harmony and a wholeness" he says he never encountered anywhere else. Many years later, reflecting on the notion of sacred geography and the human condition of being "in-between" our physical, earthly existence and our spiritual calling, he writes, "In an age when we fly at 30,000 feet and even the most banal cell phone chatter bounces off of satellites 22,000 miles into space, we have lost the sense of what heights formerly meant: liminal spots of land, places where the realm of earth encounters the realm of what's above."[7]

The Rivers, Seas, and Mountains

Conservationists, environmentalists, and those who have a strong attraction to nature tend to fall within one of three groups. The first group holds that nature, while important, is not sacred in any sense of the word. People in this profile are usually not religious. The second group believes that nature is in some way sacred, as it was created by God and thus reflects God's glory. The third group holds that nature is itself spiritual. Nature does not so much reflect God as it is God.[8] The second option is most in line with the authors' thinking and is a theme throughout this book. Nature, created by God, reflects God's glory. We can experience God in and through nature, albeit in a limited fashion. To use the language of theologians, we might say that nature or certain spots in creation are "sacramental." To put it simply, such places can have a spiritual effect on a person. Heaven is a place and a sense of being.

Two geographical locations that seem to have a very strong grip on our religious sensibilities are bodies of water and mountains.[9] Rivers, lakes, streams, and seas as well as hills and mountains can have a certain power over us. Sitting on the shores of a lake, whether in the wilderness or a beach in a great city, can enable us or prepare us to experience God's grace. The vastness of the lake, so deep, so broad, so peaceful, or the continual flow of a river can engage our spiritual sense. Water, a primeval symbol, suggests life, fertility, and prosperity. Given the many desert areas in the Middle East, it is little wonder that the authors of Genesis went into great detail to describe the four rivers of Eden.

Water, the source of life, can also be the cause of death. The story of the great flood in Genesis and Noah's ark is testimony to that fact. Water also plays a significant role in the story of Moses; as a baby he was placed in a basket and sent down the Nile River to save his life. With God's help he opened the Red Sea. On God's command he used his staff to strike a rock in the desert, instantly creating a well so that his people could drink.

If nourishment is the primary use of water, not far behind is the use of water for cleansing. The Old Testament texts speak of water in this way, and the New Testament picks up this theme with baptism. The physical action of pouring water over a person becomes the spiritual act of purifying a person.

The image of water used in the Bible is often used to describe a person, value, or power of God. The prophet Amos declares, "Let justice roll down like waters, and righteousness like an ever-flowing stream" (Amos 5:24). In a popular hymn we sing "peace like a river in my soul." And modern-day religious groups remain concerned with water. For example, in the Pacific Northwest, Catholic bishops have issued a major pastoral message on the Columbia River.[10]

Mountains and Hills

"One climbs a mountain," writes Tim Robinson, "drawn instinctively by the magnetism of the highest point, as to a summit of personal awareness, awareness of oneself as a point in relation to as much of space as can be grasped within a maximal horizon. Thus a mountain top is one of the most sensitive spots on earth."[11] After reading ancient texts, one might add that perhaps mountains are among the most spiritual spots on earth. There are more references to mountains and hills in the Bible than to any other geographical feature. The list of significant events that occurred on mountains seems endless: Noah's ark came to rest on a mountain; God tested Abraham in an incident sometimes called the "binding of Isaac" on a mountain; Moses meets God as a burning bush and is later given the Ten Commandments on a mountain; and there are several references in the Old Testament to God's holy mountain. In the New Testament, the significance of mountains continues. Jesus often goes to a mountain to pray; we refer to a famous moral teaching moment as the "Sermon on the Mount"; the miracle of the loaves and fishes happened on a mountain; the night before his death, Jesus prays on a hill, the Mount of Olives; and indeed he is finally crucified on a hill. Ultimately, his Great Commission to his disciples and ascension occur on a mountain. All of these references give some credence to the idea that mountains and hills are "thin places."

Mountains and hills reach to the heavens. Their vastness, beauty, and splendor are immeasurable. All the more impressive then is Paul's contention that "if I have all faith, so as to remove mountains, but do not have love, I am nothing" (1 Cor. 13:2). Mountains, however, are not necessarily lovely to those who must travel over them.

Others, apparently not appreciating their grandeur, have referred to mountains as the warts of the earth. Mountains present us with impenetrable, immovable, and seemingly everlasting fixtures on our physical and mental landscapes. This longevity suggests that wisdom is to be found on them. Aldo Leopold (1887–1948) describes the condition of a mountain that was so dramatic that it looked as if God had used new pruning shears to clear the brush. He demands that we take a long-term view of our relation to nature. Leopold suggests we think "like a mountain." As he notes in his regret of hunting wolves to near extinction, in *A Sand County Almanac,* "Only a mountain has lived long enough to listen objectively to the howl of a wolf."[12]

The first garden

Genesis 2:8–9

And the Lord God planted a garden in Eden, in the east; and there he put the man whom he had formed. Out of the ground the Lord God made to grow every tree that is pleasant to the sight and good for food, the tree of life also in the midst of the garden, and the tree of the knowledge of good and evil.

Jesus's places to pray

MARK 1:35

In the morning, while it was still very dark, he got up and went out to a deserted place, and there he prayed.

LUKE 4:42

At daybreak he departed and went into a deserted place. And the crowds were looking for him; and when they reached him, they wanted to prevent him from leaving them.

Leave your cabin and look around

ALCUIN

Beloved cell, retirement's sweet abode!
Farewell, a last farewell, thy poet bids thee!
Beloved cell, by smiling woods embraced,
Whose branches, shaken by the genial breeze
To meditation oft my mind disposed.
Around thee too, their health-reviving herbs
In verdure gay the fertile meadows spread;
And murmuring near, by flowery banks confined,
Through fragrant meads the crystal streamlets glide,
Wherein his nets the joyful fisher casts,
And fragrant with the apple bending bough,
With rose and lily joined, the garden's smile;
While jubilant, along thy verdant glades

93

At dawn his melody each songster pours,
And to his God attunes the notes of praise.[13]

A place of great meaning

BERNARD OF CLAIRVAUX

That spot has much charm, it greatly soothes weary minds, relieves anxieties and cares, helps souls who seek the Lord greatly to devotion, and recalls to them the thought of the heavenly sweetness towards which they aspire. The smiling countenance of the earth is painted with varying colors, the blooming verdure of spring satisfies the eyes, and its sweet odor salutes the nostrils. But while I view the flowers, while I breathe their sweet scent, the meadows recall to me the histories of ancient times; for while I drink in the sweetness of the flowers, the thought occurs to my mind of the fragrance of the clothing of the Patriarch Jacob, which the Scripture compares to the odor which mounts from a fruitful field. When I delight my eyes with the bright colors of the flowers, I am reminded that this beauty is far above that of the purple robe of Solomon, who in all his glory, could not equal the beauty of lilies of the field. . . . In this way, while I am charmed without by the sweet influence of the beauty of the country, I have not less delight within reflecting on the mysteries which are hidden beneath it.[14]

A lonely spot

Edward Abbey

At what distance should good neighbors build their houses? Let it be determined by the community's mode of travel: if by foot, four miles; if by horseback, eight miles; if by motorcar, 24 miles; if by airplane, ninety-six miles. Recall the Proverb: "Set not thy foot too often in thy neighbor's house, lest he grow weary of thee and hate thee."[15]

Ancient rhythms

Sigurd Olson

When one finally arrives at the point where schedules are forgotten, and becomes immersed in ancient rhythms, one begins to live.... On a trip long ago, I remember the first impact of a rising full moon. We were in the open on a great stretch of water, with islands in the far distance. The sky gradually brightened and an orange slice of moon appeared; we watched as the great sight unfolded before us. At that moment, the city men in the party caught a hint of its meaning. They were entranced as the moon became clear: pulsating as though alive, it rose slowly above the serrated spruces of the far shore. Then, as it almost reluctantly paled, we took to our paddles again. We searched and searched and found a long point from which we could see both sunset and moonrise at the same time. The calling of the loons meant more after that, and as the dusk settled all were aware of something new in their lives. . . . I know now as men accept the time clock of the wilderness, their lives become entirely different. It is one of the great compensations of primitive experience, and when one finally reaches the point where days are governed by daylight and dark, rather than by schedules, where one eats if hungry and sleeps when tired, and becomes completely immersed in the ancient rhythms, then one begins to live. . . . It is not surprising city dwellers leave their homes each weekend and head for beaches, mountains, or plains where they can recapture the feeling of timelessness. It is this need, as much as scenery or just getting out of town, that is the reason for their escape. In the process, however, they may still be so imbued with the sense of hurry and the thrill of travel that they actually lose what they came to find.[16]

Listen

THOMAS MERTON

What a thing it is to sit absolutely alone, in the forest, at night, cherished by this wonderful, unintelligible, perfectly innocent speech, the most comforting speech in the world, the talk that rain makes by itself all over the ridges, and the talk of the watercourses everywhere in the hollows!

Nobody started it, nobody is going to stop it. It will talk as long as it wants, this rain. As long as it talks I am going to listen.[17]

Be silent

MOTHER TERESA OF CALCUTTA

We need to find God, and he cannot be found in noise and restlessness. God is the friend of silence. See how nature—trees, flowers, grass—grows in silence; see the stars, the moon and the sun, how they move in silence . . . The more we receive in silent prayer, the more we can give in our active life. We need silence.[18]

An act of faith

CANADIAN CONFERENCE OF CATHOLIC BISHOPS

Each one of us is called to deepen our capacity to appreciate the wonders of nature as an act of faith and love. In the silence of contemplation, nature speaks of the beauty of the Creator. "If you look at the world with a pure heart, you too will see the face of God" (cf. Matt. 5:8). Standing in awe of creation can assist us to perceive the natural world as a bearer of divine grace.[19]

The spirit rolls along

ANNIE DILLARD

I have always been sympathetic with the early notion of a divine power that exists in a particular place, or that travels about over the face of the earth as a man might wander—when he is "there" he is surely not here. You can shake the hand of a man you meet in the woods; but the spirit seems to roll along like the mythical hoop snake with its tail in its mouth.[20]

Tinker Creek

ANNIE DILLARD

I live by a creek, Tinker Creek, in a valley in Virginia's Blue Ridge. . . . The creeks—Tinker and Carvin's—are an active mystery, fresh every minute. Theirs is the mystery of the continuous creation and all that providence implies: the uncertainty of vision, the horror of the fixed, the dissolution of the present, the intricacy of beauty, the pressure of fecundity, the elusiveness of the free, and the flawed nature of perfection.[21]

Hollins Pond

ANNIE DILLARD

I would like to learn, or remember, how to live. I come to Hollins Pond not so much to learn how to live as, frankly, to forget about it. That is, I don't think I can learn from a wild animal how to live in particular . . . but I might learn something of mindlessness, something of the purity of living in the physical senses and the dignity of living without bias or motive. The weasel lives in necessity and we live in choice, hating necessity and dying at the last ignobly in its talons. I would like to live as I should. . . . And I suspect that for me the way is like the weasel's: open to time and death painlessly, noticing everything, remembering nothing, choosing the given with a fierce and pointed will.[22]

Clew Bay

JAMES SILAS ROGERS

One summer—it was 1975, when I was a willfully drifting college student—I visited Ireland for the first time. I arrived there after two weeks of hitchhiking in Scotland, a country that completely caught me off guard by its beauty and its history. Ireland was in some ways disappointing; I had imagined it as being more beautiful than it turned out to be. It took me a while to realize that, while Scotland's majestic scenery amounted to one symphonic crescendo after another, Ireland is better understood as a sweet but unforgettable folk melody.

Hitchhiking through County Mayo I arrived in the little town of Newport. Croagh Patrick, a mountain that is a pilgrimage site, stands behind the town. I decided I needed to stay put for a few days, so I pitched my tent in an oak-filled campground that overlooked Clew Bay with its 365 islands.

My days at Clew Bay were both empty and strangely full; actually, most of my time there consisted of sitting on the shore, walking around the town, visiting the graveyard, and killing time until the evening when it reached a seemly hour to go to a pub and get drunk. But it was one of those unencumbered spans we rarely get as adults, or even as young people—a time when the deeper soul can at last have a chance to re-tune itself. And waiting around at Clew Bay is not like waiting in a bus station or hanging around the airport for a delayed flight, not like waiting with your thumb out for a ride. The area was charged with a harmony and a wholeness that I have never encountered elsewhere. I'm sure a hundred places in Ireland make better postcards, but it was, nonetheless, a beauty-haunted landscape. I've heard people say of the Greek islands that if you spend a little time there, you realize that some sort of god is present. The same thing was going on at Clew Bay. In the town, a shopkeeper who sold me an apple said that the early Irish monks had a tradition of going island to island, spending a day in prayer on each one for a whole year's time. The ghosts of those monks hung in the air and in the light. That Sunday, I went to Mass. It was tedious; by no stretch could I claim that I was given faith at that point. But in this seaside village, some impediment to faith was removed; I was able, as Simone Weil says, to play the believing game.

Because of that experience, I could not be as dismissive of the faith and tradition into which I had been born. I am convinced that a sacred geography was at work. When I crawled out of my little orange pup tent to spend a day looking at the bay, I was stepping near to something supernatural.[23]

Hymn to matter

PIERRE TEILHARD DE CHARDIN

Blessed be you, harsh matter, barren soil, stubborn rock: you who yield only to violence, you who force us to work if we would eat. Blessed be you, perilous matter, violent sea, untamable passion: you who unless we fetter you will devour us. . . .

Without you, without your onslaughts, without your uprootings of us, we should remain all our lives inert, stagnant, puerile, ignorant both of ourselves and of God. You who batter and then dress our wounds, you who resist us and yield to us, you who wreck and build, you who shackle and liberate, the sap of our souls, the hand of God, the flesh of Christ: it is you, matter, that I bless.[24]

The rivers in Eden

GENESIS 2:10–15

A river flows out of Eden to water the garden, and from there it divides and becomes four branches. The name of the first is Pishon; it is the one that flows around the whole land of Havilah, where there is gold; and the gold of that land is good; bdellium and onyx stone are there. The name of the second river is Gihon; it is the one that flows around the whole land of Cush. The name of the third river is Tigris, which flows east of Assyria. And the fourth river is the Euphrates.

The LORD God took the man and put him in the garden of Eden to till it and keep it.

Where the baby Moses hid

EXODUS 2:5–6

The daughter of Pharaoh came down to bathe at the river, while her attendants walked beside the river. She saw the basket among the reeds and sent her maid to bring it. When she opened it, she saw the child. He was crying, and she took pity on him. "This must be one of the Hebrews' children," she said.

When Buddha entered Nirvana

BUDDHIST SCRIPTURES

And when the Sage entered Nirvana, the earth quivered like a ship struck by a squall, and firebrands fell from the sky. The heavens were lit up by a preternatural fire, which burned without fuel, without smoke, without being fanned by the wind. Fearsome thunderbolts crashed down on the earth, and violent winds raged in the sky. The moon's light waned, and, in spite of a cloudless sky, an uncanny darkness spread everywhere. The rivers, as if overcome with grief, were filled with boiling water. Beautiful flowers grew out of season on the Sal trees above the Buddha's couch, and the trees bent down over him and showered his golden body with their flowers.[25]

A good person is like a tree planted near water

PSALM 1:3 (ESV)

He is like a tree planted by streams of water that yields its fruit in its season, and its leaf does not wither. In all that he does, he prospers.

You shower the earth

PSALM 65:7–13

You silence the roaring of the seas, the roaring of their waves, the tumult of the peoples.

Those who live at earth's farthest bounds are awed by your signs; you make the gateways of the morning and the evening shout for joy.

You visit the earth and water it, you greatly enrich it; the river of God is full of water; you provide the people with grain, for so you have prepared it.

You water its furrows abundantly, settling its ridges, softening it with showers, and blessing its growth.

You crown the year with your bounty; your wagon tracks overflow with richness.

The pastures of the wilderness overflow, the hills gird themselves with joy, the meadows clothe themselves with flocks, the valleys deck themselves with grain, they shout and sing together for joy.

God rules the sea

PSALM 89:8–9

O LORD God of hosts, who is as mighty as you, O LORD? Your faithfulness surrounds you.

You rule the raging of the sea; when its waves rise, you still them.

The good king

ISAIAH 32:1–2

See, a king will reign in righteousness, and princes will rule with justice. Each will be like a hiding place from the wind, a covert from the tempest, like streams of water in a dry place, like the shade of a great rock in a weary land.

I give water to my people

ISAIAH 43:19–21

I am about to do a new thing; now it springs forth, do you not perceive it? I will make a way in the wilderness and rivers in the desert. The wild animals will honor me, the jackals and the ostriches; for I give water in the wilderness, rivers in the desert, to give drink to my chosen people, the people whom I formed for myself so that they might declare my praise.

Righteousness

ISAIAH 48:18–19

O that you had paid attention to my commandments! Then your prosperity would have been like a river, and your success like the waves of the sea; your offspring would have been like the sand, and your descendants like its grains; their name would never be cut off or destroyed from before me.

Where rivers go

ECCLESIASTES 1:7

All streams run to the sea, but the sea is not full; to the place where the streams flow, there they continue to flow.

Autumn floods

CHUANG TZU, SECTION 17

Of all the waters of the world, none is as great as the sea. Ten thousand streams flow into it—I have never heard of a time when they stopped—and yet it is never full. The water leaks away at Wei-lü—I have never heard a time that it didn't—and yet the sea is never empty. Spring or autumn, it never changes. Flood or drought, it takes no notice.[26]

The power of God at the shore

JEREMIAH 5:22

Do you not fear me? says the LORD; Do you not tremble before me? I placed the sand as a boundary for the sea, a perpetual barrier that it cannot pass; though the waves toss, they cannot prevail, though they roar, they cannot pass over it.

False teachers

JUDE 1:12–13

These are blemishes on your love-feasts, while they feast with you without fear, feeding themselves. They are waterless clouds carried along by the winds; autumn trees without fruit, twice dead, uprooted; wild waves of the sea, casting up the foam of their own shame; wandering stars, for whom the deepest darkness has been reserved forever.

Wash in the river

2 KINGS 5:10

Elisha sent a messenger to him, saying, "Go, wash in the Jordan seven times, and your flesh shall be restored and you shall be clean."

John's baptisms

MATTHEW 3:5–6

Then the people of Jerusalem and all Judea were going out to him, and all the region along the Jordan, and they were baptized by him in the river Jordan, confessing their sins.

Holy Spirit and living water

JOHN 7:37–38

On the last day of the festival, the great day, while Jesus was standing there, he cried out, "Let anyone who is thirsty come to me, and let the one who believes in me drink. As the scripture has said, 'Out of the believer's heart shall flow rivers of living water.'"

The ark came to rest

GENESIS 8:3–4

. . . and the waters gradually receded from the earth. At the end of one hundred fifty days the waters had abated; and in the seventh month, on the seventeenth day of the month, the ark came to rest on the mountains of Ararat.

Up the mountain to God

EXODUS 19:2–6

They had journeyed from Rephidim, entered the wilderness of Sinai, and camped in the wilderness; Israel camped there in front of the mountain. Then Moses went up to God; the Lord called to him from the mountain, saying, "Thus you shall say to the house of Jacob, and tell the Israelites: You have seen what I did to the Egyptians, and how I bore you on eagles' wings and brought you to myself. Now therefore, if you obey my voice and keep my covenant, you shall be my treasured possession out of all the peoples. Indeed, the whole earth is mine, but you shall be for me a priestly kingdom and a holy nation. These are the words that you shall speak to the Israelites."

The death of Moses

DEUTERONOMY 34:1–7

Then Moses went up from the plains of Moab to Mount Nebo, to the top of Pisgah, which is opposite Jericho, and the LORD showed him the whole land: Gilead as far as Dan, all Naphtali, the land of Ephraim and Manasseh, all the land of Judah as far as the Western Sea, the Negeb, and the Plain—that is, the valley of Jericho, the city of palm trees—as far as Zoar. The Lord said to him, "This is the land of which I swore to Abraham, to Isaac, and to Jacob, saying, 'I will give it to your descendants'; I have let you see it with your eyes, but you shall not cross over there." Then Moses, the servant of the LORD, died there in the land of Moab, at the Lord's command. He was buried in a valley in the land of Moab, opposite Beth-peor, but no one knows his burial place to this day. Moses was one hundred twenty years old when he died; his sight was unimpaired and his vigor had not abated.

The mountains and offerings to God

JOSHUA 8:30–33

Then Joshua built on Mount Ebal an altar to the LORD, the God of Israel, just as Moses the servant of the LORD had commanded the Israelites, as it is written in the book of the law of Moses, "an altar of unhewn stones, on which no iron tool has been used"; and they offered on it burnt offerings to the LORD, and sacrificed offerings of well-being. And there, in the presence of the Israelites, Joshua wrote on the stones a copy of the law of Moses, which he had written. All Israel, alien as well as citizen, with their elders and officers and their judges, stood on opposite sides of the ark in front of the levitical priests who carried the ark of the covenant of the LORD, half of them in front of Mount Gerizim and half of them in front of Mount Ebal, as Moses the servant of the LORD had commanded at the first, that they should bless the people of Israel.

Mountains break into song

ISAIAH 55:12–13 AND 44:23

For you shall go out in joy, and be led back in peace; the mountains and the hills before you shall burst into song, and all the trees of the field shall clap their hands. Instead of the thorn shall come up the cypress; instead of the brier shall come up the myrtle; and it shall be to the LORD for a memorial, for an everlasting sign that shall not be cut off.

Sing, O heavens, for the LORD has done it; shout, O depths of the earth; break forth into singing, O mountains, O forest, and every tree in it!

Jesus and mountains

MATTHEW 4:8–10

Again, the devil took him to a very high mountain and showed him all the kingdoms of the world and their splendor; and he said to him, "All these I will give you, if you will fall down and worship me." Jesus said to him, "Away with you, Satan! for it is written, 'Worship the Lord your God, and serve only him.'"

MATTHEW 5:1–2

When Jesus saw the crowds, he went up the mountain; and after he sat down, his disciples came to him. Then he began to speak, and taught them . . .

MATTHEW 14:23

And after he had dismissed the crowds, he went up the mountain by himself to pray. When evening came, he was there alone . . .

MATTHEW 17:1–2

Six days later, Jesus took with him Peter and James and his brother John and led them up a high mountain, by themselves. And he was transfigured before them, and his face shone like the sun, and his clothes became dazzling white.

LUKE 9:28–29

Now about eight days after these sayings Jesus took with him Peter and John and James, and went up on the mountain to pray. And while he was praying, the appearance of his face changed, and his clothes became dazzling white.

MARK 6:46

After saying farewell to them, he went up on the mountain to pray.

LUKE 6:12

Now during those days he went out to the mountain to pray; and he spent the night in prayer to God.

Refreshing the soul

RICHARD JEFFERIES

There were times every now and then when I felt the necessity of a strong inspiration of soul-thought. My heart was dusty, parched for want of the rain of deep feeling; my mind arid and dry, for there is a dust which settles on the heart as well as that which falls on a ledge. It is injurious to the mind as well as to the body to be always in one place and always surrounded by the same circumstances. I felt eager to escape from it, to throw it off like heavy clothing, to drink deeply once more at the fresh fountains of life. An inspiration—a long deep breath of the pure air of thought—could alone give health to the heart.

There was a hill to which I used to resort at such periods. The labour of walking three miles to it, all the while gradually ascending, seemed to clear my blood of the heaviness accumulated at home. On a warm summer day the slow continued rise required continual effort, which carried away the sense of oppression. The familiar everyday scene was soon out of sight; I came to other trees, meadows, and fields; I began to breathe a new air and to have a fresher aspiration. I restrained my soul till I reached the sward of the hill; psyche, the soul that longed to be loose. . . .

Moving up the sweet short turf, at every step my heart seemed to obtain a wider horizon of feeling; with every inhalation of rich pure air, a deeper desire. The very light of the sun was whiter and more brilliant here. By the time I had reached the summit I had entirely forgotten the petty circumstances and the annoyances of existence. I felt myself, myself. . . .

I was utterly alone with the sun and the earth. Lying down on the grass, I spoke in my soul to the earth, the sun, the air, and the distant sea far beyond sight. I thought of the earth's firmness—I felt it bear me up; through the grassy couch there came an influence as if I could feel the great earth speaking to me. I thought of the wandering air—its pureness, which is its beauty; the air touched me and gave me something of itself. I spoke to the sea: though so far, in my mind I saw it, green at the rim of the earth and blue in deeper ocean; I desired to have its strength, its mystery and glory. Then I addressed the sun, desiring the soul equivalent of his light and brilliance, his endurance and unwearied race. I turned to the blue heaven over, gazing into its depth, inhaling its exquisite colour and sweetness. The rich blue of the unattainable flower of the sky drew my soul towards it, and there it rested, for pure colour is rest of heart. By these I prayed.[27]

The highest mountain

CHIEF BLACK ELK

Then I was standing on the highest mountain of them all, and round about beneath me was the whole hoop of the world. And while I stood there I saw more than I can tell and I understood more than I saw; for I was seeing in a sacred manner the shapes of all things in the spirit, and the shape of all shapes as they must live together like one being.

And I saw the sacred hoop of my people was one of the many hoops that made one circle, wide as daylight and as starlight, and in the center grew one mighty flowering tree to shelter all the children of one mother and one father. And I saw that it was holy. . . .

But anywhere is the center of the world.[28]

Majesty of the mountains

POPE JOHN PAUL II

I love these mountains; up here one breathes with the pure mountain air the mysterious invitation to faith and conversion. . . . In front of the majesty of the mountains we are pushed to establish a more respectful relationship with nature. . . . At the same time . . . we are stimulated to meditate upon the gravity of so many desecrations of nature, often carried out with inadmissible nonchalance.[29]

These mountains

ANNIE DILLARD

I came here to study hard things—rock mountain and salt sea—and to temper my spirit on their edges. "Teach me thy ways, O Lord" is, like all prayers, a rash one, and one I cannot but recommend. These mountains—Mount Baker and the Sisters and Shuksan, the Canadian Coastal Range and the Olympics on the peninsula—are surely the edge of the known and comprehended world. . . . That they bear their own unimaginable masses and weathers aloft, holding them up in the sky for anyone to see plain, makes them, as Chesterton said of the Eucharist, only the more mysterious by their very visibility and absence of secrecy.[30]

Celtic blessing

FIONA MCLEOD

Deep peace, pure white of the moon to you;
Deep peace, pure green of the grass to you;
Deep peace, pure brown of the earth to you;
Deep peace, pure grey of the dew to you;
Deep peace, pure blue of the sky to you;
Deep peace of the running wave to you;
Deep peace of the flowing air to you;
Deep peace of the quiet earth to you;
Deep peace of the shining stars to you;
Deep peace of the Son of Peace to you.[31]

116

4

Into the Wilderness

People head into the wilderness—the word derives from an old English term meaning "the place of wild beasts"—for many reasons, not all of which are overtly spiritual or religious. They hope to, perhaps, get away from the crowds and the daily noise that cloud their lives. Some people go into the woods or out on the lake to remove themselves from comforts and indeed the temptations of everyday life. People go out-of-doors to get some fresh air so as to, in a sense, purify themselves. Trips into the desert or hiking through a forest may simply be a form of exercise for some, yet there is more to these experiences than a brisk walk through the mall. This chapter invites you to explore the spiritual signifi-

117

cance of cross-country skiing in the woods or a canoe ride "away from it all."

Wilderness and the Bible

There are two very significant trips into the wilderness in the Bible. The first is found in the Old Testament, the story of which takes up four of the first five books of the Bible: Exodus, Leviticus, Numbers, and Deuteronomy. It is the story of Moses leading the Israelites from slavery in Egypt to the Promised Land of Canaan. The readings tell of the back-and-forth relationship between God and the people. The accounts of forty years' wandering in the desert could be considered the first Judeo-Christian travel narrative. The people experienced the "great and terrible" elements of the wilderness (Deut. 1:19). But God provided for them, guided them, and tested them. Indeed, the wilderness was a place of temptation for them (Ps. 106:4) as they themselves tested, sinned, and rebelled against God (Ps. 78). Like many journeys, the Israelites' was filled with great joy and sorrow, with danger and reward. The image was enduring enough for Thomas Jefferson to suggest that the first seal of the United States, in 1776, should contain an image of the children of Israel being led through the wilderness; he lost out to *E pluribus unum*, which was Benjamin Franklin's idea.[1]

The other famous biblical trip into the wilderness is recorded in the Gospels of Matthew, Mark, and Luke. Jesus goes into the wilderness for forty days as a preparation for his public ministry. The only details the Gospel writers mention of this time was that Jesus was tempted by the devil. Luke (4:1–13) writes that Jesus was tempted to use his power for his own self-interest, for example, to "command this stone to become a loaf of bread"; he was tempted to possess "all the kingdoms of the world" and to test his relationship with God: "If you are the Son of God, throw yourself down." The wilderness becomes the place where Jesus meets and beats the devil. He is a stronger person when he returns to collect his disciples.

Trips into wilderness, whether they are forty minutes, forty days, or forty years, test us. They can help us find out "what we are made of." They can tempt us. They can make us stronger. And, of course, the "wild" can be a dangerous place as well as a beautiful place. Indeed, that is one of the reasons people today spend time in the wilderness. Going off into nature can be a metaphor; we often hear the phrase "to find myself." This is not be understood in a selfish sense, but as a time for reflection on who one is and one's place in the world. Sometimes the challenges of the wilderness are the terrible beauties of nature: wind, rain, snow, cold, insects, and animals. At other times the challenges of the wilderness can be found in the peace of the woods. We have to face ourselves. There should be no TV or radio or cell phone or pager or video game or CD player to distract us.

In all four Gospels, truth comes from the wilderness. Matthew, Mark, Luke, and John all include the story of Jesus's precursor, John the Baptist. They all write that John quotes the prophet Isaiah (40:3) as he announces the imminent coming of Jesus. "I am the voice of one crying out in the wilderness, make straight the way of the Lord" (John 1:23; see also Matt. 3:3; Mark 1:3; Luke 3:4).

To Communicate with God

The Gospels tell us that on several occasions Jesus went into the wilderness to pray. Christians and others throughout the ages have imitated this behavior (knowingly or not) and, like Jesus, have traveled to the desert or sat by the lake or hiked up the mountain to pray. Why is that? Why have spiritual seekers from the earliest times set off into the wild to communicate with their spiritual leader? Perhaps it is the beauty of and our vulnerability in the face of nature that inspires us. Maybe it is the quiet and solitude of nature that is inviting. The experience of nature, particularly when not threatening and dangerous, can be regenerative. James Nash writes that people throughout history "have been filled with awe and wonder, moved to humility and contemplation, perplexed by the paradox of holistic order through brutal predation, overpowered by a sense of mystery, and yet strangely grasped by the consciousness of God's loving presence."[2] In a similar vein, David R. Williams writes, "It is not possible to read the Bible without being impressed by the importance of the experience of God's people in the wilderness to the writers of scripture."[3]

The Bible is overflowing with images of water in the desert or gardens in the desert. The idea that wilderness could be a place to cleanse oneself from sin, or to shield oneself from temptation, or to become strengthened and replenished is found in places as diverse as Native American sweat lodge ceremonies and the ancient Christian monasteries located on the fringes of civilization. According to Ulrich Mauser, in the Old Testament, wilderness is a basic symbol of repentance, a rejection of sinful ways, and "the stage that brightly illuminates God's power."[4] Throughout history, hermits, monks, and other religious have sought wilderness as place of refuge and divine revelation.

———•◦•———

Going off into nature to seek God is a fairly typical occurrence for early American authors. Jonathan Edwards, Ralph Waldo Emerson, and Emily Dickinson, for example, each embraced solitude in nature as a way to encounter God.

Edwards, a Protestant preacher and perhaps the most important early American theologian, writes in 1740 about "appearance of divine glory in almost every thing . . . in the grass, flowers, trees; in the water, and all nature."[5] Similarly, Emerson, some hundred years later, wrote, "In the garden, the eye watches the flying cloud and distant woods but turns from the village."[6] Dickinson in 1856 described "the crumbling elms and evergreens—and other crumbling things—that spring and fade . . . well they are here, and skies . . . in blue eye look down . . . a league from here, on the way to Heaven!"[7]

Many Native American traditions include trips into the wilderness. One of the remarkable lives of the twentieth century was lived by Florence Curl Jones (1907–2003). Jones (also known as Puilulimet) was a member of the Winnemem Wintu tribe of the western United States. Florence's mother was said to have been nearly sixty years old when she was born; tribal elders gathered to determine whether the baby was good or bad—they decided she was good, and she was trained in the healing arts and in tribal culture and language.

When she was ten years old, Florence was sent by the tribe on an eighty-mile, one-week hike into the Mount Shasta area, as a coming-of-age ritual. Alone in the northern California wilderness, she completed the trip successfully. As she grew into adulthood, Florence became an important political activist for the preservation of Indian lands and language. She helped preserve areas of Mount Shasta, which is in the Cascade Range where her tribe's native lands are located.

Despite the examples of early American authors and Native Americans, one of the lasting impressions from reading many modern accounts of (mostly men) heading off into the wilderness is the lack of a spiritual element as a reason for their quest. The mountaineering writer David Roberts noted that "super climbers," those men who risk their lives to summit the world's greatest peaks, have a hard time articulating why they climb, but "love of nature, by the way, seems to have little to do with it."[8] A spiritual quest or a supreme being is hardly ever mentioned. Religion is noteworthy enough to Roberts to make mention of a climber named Layton Kor, who, after finding the body of a friend at the base of a mountain, dropped out of sight and became a Jehovah's Witness.[9]

Then there are those twentieth-century wilderness authors who stand apart from those who ignore or simply don't think about spiritual aspects of their wilderness experiences. Sigurd Olson noted, "Life in the wilderness, especially when one is alone, is a continual contemplation and communion with God and Spirit regarding eternal values."[10] For Olson, the outdoors was a place to find peace, happiness, and quiet. And, for him, the trips often were about God—meeting God on his terms, or more accurately, on his turf. Similarly, John Haines (1924–)

lived for more than twenty years as a homesteader in Alaska; as a poet and a memoirist, he related the frontier experience to his twentieth-century readers. He is able in a few words to capture the personal and interpersonal significance of the wilderness for people. His hunting, trapping, dog sledding, and the rest were a part of what he called "the inmost human experience on this earth."[11]

But, as Olson and Haines well recognized, and the writers of Genesis and Job mention, nature is not without its dangers, great and small. "It ain't wilderness," wrote Edward Abbey, quoting an eco-warrior friend, "unless there's a critter out there that can kill you and eat you."[12] The ancients, in describing the awesome power of God, often use the strong and sometimes violent and destructive actions of nature. Job speaks of storms and stars and lightning; Martin Luther (1483–1546) noted God's creations that seem less than wonderful—fleas, thistles, and the like—and saw them as a reminder of sin. To Luther, one result of original sin meant that all creatures were no longer peacefully coexisting with humans. In Eden, plants were the only food. The creation of carnivores kicks in with the fall.

————•—

The American Puritans also saw the awesome power of God everywhere. Anne Bradstreet (ca. 1612–1672), considered by many as America's first woman poet, was

Puritan to her roots but understood the power of nature and its symbols of God. Cotton Mather (1663–1728), another Puritan, also reflects his religion's ideas about the nature of God and divine punishment. The spiritual maxim "Find God in all things" is nowhere clearer than in the Old Testament texts that discuss seeing God in nature. Isaiah describes God's coming as in a firelike whirlwind (Is. 66:15); yet First Kings notes that God came to Elijah not as a strong wind or an earthquake or a fire, but in a small voice.

Psalm 23—"Tho I walk through the valley of darkness"—in just a few lines captures the essence of faith, hope, and confidence we have in God's love for us. The idea of a pasture—where humans and animals can rest and find respite—and of course the words *pastoral* and *pastor* all come from the Latin *pastus,* past participle of *pascere,* which means "to feed." Gene Stratton Porter (1863–1924) recognized the importance of pasture; she was an advocate for nature before such a job existed. A writer and naturalist, she grew up on the banks of the storied Wabash River in Indiana. Porter wrote eleven novels, two children's books, seven nature studies, and many poems and magazine articles. In an unhappy irony for a lover of nature, she died of injuries in a most urban

125

way—injuries suffered in an automobile accident in Los Angeles in 1924.

On Pilgrimage

A recurring theme in Judeo-Christian spirituality is the journey or pilgrimage. Two key themes stand out in the history of spiritual literature on pilgrimage: the destination and the journey. We can define *pilgrimage* as a trip to a holy place, a devotional journey motivated by the desire to seek penance, to offer thanksgiving, or to ask for divine assistance. There are thousands of sites in Europe alone that attract millions of pilgrims each year. Loreto, Italy, for example, is said to contain the remains of a dwelling (Holy House) where Jesus lived; believers from all over the world come to pay homage there.[13] Elsewhere in the world, Mohammed's birthplace in the western Saudi Arabian city of Mecca attracts thousands of Muslim worshipers each day; every Muslim is supposed to go at least once in his or her life. Two million people gather there for ten days each year to commemorate key events in Islam. Indeed the very name of the community has become the word for a place that is the center for an activity or interest. Similarly, the Ganges River in India is a sacred place to Hindus.

Yet the true "destination" of a pilgrimage is not necessarily a sacred place. A pilgrimage can be thought of as

126

a journey to an inner destination. In seeking the divine, one often finds a new or renewed self. Another view of a pilgrimage is that it is not so much the destination that matters as does the trip itself and the relationship with one's companions along the way. An ancient Irish proverb captures the notion that it is the intention, the motivation, and indeed the journey itself that counts in a pilgrimage, and not simply the destination: "Who to Rome goes, much labor, little profit knows; For God, on earth though long you've sought him, you'll miss at Rome unless you've brought him." The popular *Lord of the Rings* books and movies capture this notion of a journey as a spiritual quest. Life is not only about where you are going, but what you do and whom you meet along the way.

An Irish monk, Brendan the Voyager (ca. 484–583) took one of the most famous journeys to wild places in Christian history. Although the details have been debated for years, the basic story has Brendan and many fellow monks on a multiyear voyage in a long, narrow, wood-and-ox-hide single-mast boat or boats called carraughs (or curraghs). The travelers, using wind power from a lone sail and oars during calm days, stowed wine and cold food for their journeys over the North Atlantic, and they possibly reached Iceland. The crew, in sort of a "floating monastery," suffered the usual hardships, but also saw ecstatic visions, experienced healings, and searched to discover the Isles of the Blessed or the Island of Promise.[14] Two accounts of these trips were published, one in the

127

eighth or ninth century and one in the twelfth century, although the original text has been lost for the latter account. According to the texts, Brendan's trips lasted from seven to nine years and included up to seventeen monks, including a few who died along the way.

Brendan dedicated his command to the Holy Trinity, which one maritime historian, George Little, has called the earliest example of the "christening" of a ship. Perhaps the most famous story of Brendan's experience came when, after weeks of sailing, the crew happened upon a tiny islet, so small it did not have a bay, a tree, a shrub, or so much as a flower. The day was Easter.

At the conclusion of the Easter service, the crew prepared for whatever holiday feast it could muster. Brendan stood apart from the rest, near the carraugh. A blazing fire was lit and the pot set to boil. The wind caught the flames and whipped the fire red-hot; the island shuddered and began to sink. Terror-stricken, the crew panicked but Brendan calmed them, shepherded them safely into the boat, and struggled away. The monks had celebrated Easter Mass on the back of a living, sleeping whale.

Recreation Means Re-creation

Perhaps the main reason people leave the busy world and head into the woods is for recreation. But what does recreation mean but to re-create the self, to refresh the self, to restore what was lost or forgotten? A contemporary writer, Gretel Ehrlich (1946–), has earned the reputation as the "Whitman of Wyoming." Her writing, like Walt Whitman's poems, links images from nature to patterns in and processes in one's life. Pope John Paul II captured the connection between contact with nature, self-reflection, and the voice of God when he wrote about the restorative power of wilderness. The prolific, award-winning writer Barbara Kingsolver (1955–) laments how much we lose by living in large urban areas and reminds us of the human need for wilderness.

A final introductory remark is in order. The fundamental point of this chapter is to suggest that physical objects—trees, water, stars, dirt—can lead us to transcendence and to the Transcendent. Stepping outside our normal situations can charge us with the possibility to see these situations from a new, more comprehensive, view. A simple walk in the woods is not simply a walk in the woods.

Wilderness tests us

DEUTERONOMY 8:2–10

Remember the long way that the LORD your God has led you these forty years in the wilderness, in order to humble you, testing you to know what was in your heart, whether or not you would keep his commandments. He humbled you by letting you hunger, then by feeding you with manna, with which neither you nor your ancestors were acquainted, in order to make you understand that one does not live by bread alone, but by every word that comes from the mouth of the Lord. The clothes on your back did not wear out and your feet did not swell these forty years. Know then in your heart that as a parent disciplines a child so the Lord your God disciplines you. Therefore keep the commandments of the Lord your God, by walking in his ways and by fearing him. For the Lord your God is bringing you into a good land, a land with flowing streams, with springs and underground waters welling up in valleys and hills, a land of wheat and barley, of vines and fig trees and pomegranates, a land of olive trees and honey, a land where you may eat bread without scarcity, where you will lack nothing, a land whose stones are iron and from whose hills you may mine copper. You shall eat your fill and bless the Lord your God for the good land that he has given you.

Led into the wilderness

Luke 4:1

Jesus, full of the Holy Spirit, returned from the Jordan and was led by the Spirit in the wilderness . . .

Getting away to the beach

MATTHEW 13:1

That same day Jesus went out of the house and sat beside the sea.

God in the wilderness

BRENDAN THE NAVIGATOR

Do not fear. God will be of our crew, be at our helm, act as our pilot. Ship sweeps. Leave set the sail. We are His company, this His ship. May He use us all to His will.[15]

The reason for the journey

BARRY LOPEZ

Walking along the beach, remembering Brendan's deference and Parry's and Davis's voyages, I could only think what exquisite moments these must have been. Inescapable hardship transcended by a desire for spiritual elevation, or the desire to understand, to comprehend what lay in darkness.[16]

131

Look around on the way

ROBERT PIRSIG

Mountains should be climbed with as little effort as possible and without desire. . . . Then, when you're no longer thinking ahead, each footstep isn't just a means to an end but a unique event in itself . . . to live for some future goal is shallow. It's the sides of the mountain which sustain life, not the top. Here's where things grow.[17]

On nature and the soul

FLORENCE CURL JONES (PUILULIMET)

Nature takes care of your mind, and your heart and soul. This is my church.[18]

Share experiences with others

SIGURD OLSON

I believe as long as we have only one life to live, it is a pity not to share it with others. Wilderness can be appreciated only by contrast, and solitude understood only when we have been without it. We cannot separate ourselves from society, comradeship, sharing, and love. Unless we can contribute something from wilderness experience, derive some solace of peace to share with others, then the real purpose is defeated.[19]

Communion with nature

SIGURD OLSON

Life in the wilderness can be a continual contemplation and communion with God and Spirit of those values echoing within us all, values born of timelessness, mystery, the great silences, and an ancient way of life.[20]

Life without meaning

SIGURD OLSON

In the wilderness there is never this sense of having to move, never the feeling of boredom if nothing dramatic happens. Time moves slowly, as it should, for it is a part of beauty that cannot be hurried if it is to be understood. Without this easy flowing, life can become empty and hectic. . . . We cannot all live in the wilderness, or even close to it, but we can, no matter where we spend our lives, remember the background which shaped this sense of the eternal rhythm, remember that days, no matter how frenzied their pace, can be calm and unhurried. Knowing we can be calm and unhurried, we can refuse to be caught in the so-called rat race and the tension, which kills God-like leisure. Though conscious of the roar around us, we can find peace if we remember we all came from a common mold and primeval background. It is when we forget and divorce ourselves entirely from what man once knew that our lives may spin off without meaning.[21]

In search of something

JOHN HAINES

Who comes here, to this whiteness, this far and frozen place, in search of something he cannot name? Not wealth, it may be, but a fortune of the spirit, a freshness denied him in the place he came from. The North glitters and brightens; the land grows dark again, and the fugitive glow from a gas mantle lights the shadows.[22]

Difficulties on the journey

GENESIS 3:17–19

And to the man he said, "Because you have listened to the voice of your wife, and have eaten of the tree about which I commanded you, 'You shall not eat of it,' cursed is the ground because of you; in toil you shall eat of it all the days of your life; thorns and thistles it shall bring forth for you; and you shall eat the plants of the field. By the sweat of your face you shall eat bread until you return to the ground, for out of it you were taken; you are dust, and to dust you shall return."

The consequences of original sin

Martin Luther

Just as Adam and Eve acknowledged God as their Lord, so later on they themselves ruled over the other creatures in the air, in the water, and on the earth.[23]

If Adam had not fallen into sin, wolves, lions, and bears would not have acquired their well-known savage disposition. Absolutely nothing in the entire creation would have been either troublesome or harmful for man.[24]

If man had not sinned, all the beasts would have remained obedient.[25]

I believe that Adam [before he sinned] could command a lion with a single word, just as we give a command to a trained dog.[26]

Our body bears the traces of God's wrath, which our sin has deserved. God's wrath also appears on the earth in all creatures. And yet we look at all these things with a smug and unconcerned attitude! And what of thorns, thistles, water, fire, caterpillars, flies, fleas, and bedbugs? Collectively and individually, are not all of them messengers who preach to us concerning sin and God's wrath, since they did not exist before sin or at least were not harmful and troublesome?[27]

Satan's hook

ANNE BRADSTREET

The skillful fisher hath several baits, for several fish, but there is a hook under all. Satan that great angler hath his sundry baits for sundry tempers of men, which they all catch greedily at but few perceive the hook till it be too late.[28]

On comets

COTTON MATHER

Even Comets, too, move so as to serve the Holy Ends of their Creator! . . .

When I see a vast Comet, blazing and rolling about the unmeasurable *Aether*, I will think: Who can tell, but now I see a wicked World made fiery Oven in the Time of the Anger of GOD! The Lord swallowed them up in his Wrath, and the Fire devouring them![29]

God stills the seas

PSALM 65:7–13

You silence the roaring of the seas, the roaring of their waves, the tumult of the peoples.

Those who live at earth's farthest bounds are awed by your signs; you make the gateways of the morning and the evening shout for joy.

You visit the earth and water it, you greatly enrich it; the river of God is full of water; you provide the people with grain, for so you have prepared it.

You water its furrows abundantly, settling its ridges, softening it with showers, and blessing its growth.

You crown the year with your bounty; your wagon tracks overflow with richness.

The pastures of the wilderness overflow, the hills gird themselves with joy, the meadows clothe themselves with flocks, the valleys deck themselves with grain, they shout and sing together for joy.

God in the storm

JOB 38:1, 12–13, 16–18, 22, 24–38

Then the LORD answered Job out of the whirlwind:

"Have you commanded the morning since your days began, and caused the dawn to know its place, so that it might take hold of the skirts of the earth, and the wicked be shaken out of it?

"Have you entered into the springs of the sea, or walked in the recesses of the deep? Have the gates of death been revealed to you, or have you seen the gates of deep darkness? Have you comprehended the expanse of the earth? Declare, if you know all this.

"Have you entered the storehouses of the snow, or have you seen the storehouses of the hail . . .?

"What is the way to the place where the light is distributed, or where the east wind is scattered upon the earth?

"Who has cut a channel for the torrents of rain, and a way for the thunderbolt, to bring rain on a land where no one lives, on the desert, which is empty of human life, to satisfy the waste and desolate land, and to make the ground put forth grass?

"Has the rain a father, or who has begotten the drops of dew?

"From whose womb did the ice come forth, and who has given birth to the hoarfrost of heaven?

"The waters become hard like stone, and the face of the deep is frozen.

"Can you bind the chains of the Pleiades, or loose the cords of Orion?

"Can you lead forth the Mazzaroth in their season, or can you guide the Bear with its children?

"Do you know the ordinances of the heavens? Can you establish their rule on the earth?

"Can you lift up your voice to the clouds, so that a flood of waters may cover you?

"Can you send forth lightnings, so that they may go and say to you, 'Here we are'?

"Who has put wisdom in the inward parts, or given understanding to the mind? Who has the wisdom to number the clouds? Or who can tilt the waterskins of the heavens, when the dust runs into a mass and the clods cling together?"

The call of Elijah

1 Kings 19:11–12

He said, "Go out and stand on the mountain before the Lord, for the Lord is about to pass by." Now there was a great wind, so strong that it was splitting mountains and breaking rocks in pieces before the Lord, but the Lord was not in the wind; and after the wind an earthquake, but the Lord was not in the earthquake; and after the earthquake a fire, but the Lord was not in the fire; and after the fire a sound of sheer silence.

Though I walk through a dark valley

Psalm 23

The Lord is my shepherd, I shall not want.

He makes me lie down in green pastures; he leads me beside still waters; he restores my soul.

He leads me in right paths for his name's sake.

Even though I walk through the darkest valley, I fear no evil; for you are with me; your rod and your staff—they comfort me.

You prepare a table before me in the presence of my enemies; you anoint my head with oil; my cup overflows.

Surely goodness and mercy shall follow me all the days of my life, and I shall dwell in the house of the LORD my whole life long.

The meaning of pasture

GENE STRATTON PORTER

Few words of our language are more suggestive of peace and comfort than "pasture." *Pastorem,* a green feeding-ground, according to the old Latins. And wherever there is a green feeding-ground you may be sure that you will find the shade of trees and bushes, and frequently there is running water. Wherever you locate these you hear a swelling bird and insect chorus.[30]

The power and the beauty

ISAIAH 28:2, 4

See, the Lord has one who is mighty and strong; like a storm of hail, a destroying tempest, like a storm of mighty, overflowing waters; with his hand he will hurl them down to the earth.

And the fading flower of its glorious beauty, which is on the head of those bloated with rich food, will be like a first-ripe fig before the summer; whoever sees it, eats it up as soon as it comes to hand.

On water

GRETEL EHRLICH

Everything in nature invites us constantly to be what we are. We are often like rivers: careless and forceful, timid and dangerous, lucid and muddied, eddying, gleaming, still. Lovers, farmers, and artists have one thing in common, at least—a fear of "dry spells," dormant periods in which we do no blooming, internal droughts only the waters of imagination and psychic release can civilize. All such matters are delicate of course. But a good irrigator knows this: too little water brings on the weeds while too much degrades the soil the way too much easy money can trivialize a person's initiative. In his journal Thoreau wrote, "A man's life should be as fresh as a river. It should be the same channel but a new water every instant."[31]

Contact with nature restores us

POPE JOHN PAUL II

Here the silence of the mountain and the whiteness of the snow speak to us of God, and they show us the way of contemplation, not only as a way to experience the Mystery, but also as a condition for humanizing life and mutual relations.

Today there is a greatly felt need to slow down the sometimes-hectic pace of our days. Contact with nature, with its beauty and its peace, gives us new strength and restores us. Yet, while the eyes take in the wonder of the cosmos, it is necessary to look into ourselves, into the depths of our heart, into the center of our being where we are face to face with our conscience. There God speaks to us and the dialogue with Him gives meaning to our lives.

So, dear friends, . . . you are, as it were, molded by the mountain, by its beauty and its severity, by its mysteries and its attractions. The mountain opens its secrets only to those who have the courage to challenge it. It demands sacrifice and training. It requires you to leave the security of the valleys but offers spectacular views from the summit to those who have the courage to climb it. Therefore it is a reality, which strongly suggests the journey of the spirit, called to lift itself up from the earth to heaven, to meet God.[32]

Connection to nature/connection to the infinite

BARBARA KINGSOLVER

With all due respect for the wondrous ways people have invented to amuse themselves and one another on paved surfaces, I find that this exodus from the land makes me unspeakably sad. I think of the children who will never know, intuitively, that a flower is a plant's way of making love, or what silence sounds like, or that trees breathe out what we breathe in. I think of the astonished neighbor children who huddled around my husband in his tiny backyard garden, in the city where he lived years ago, clapping their hands to their mouths in pure dismay at seeing him pull *carrots* from the *ground*. (Ever the thoughtful teacher, he explained about fruits and roots and asked, "What other foods do you think might grow in the ground?" They knit their brows, conferred, and offered brightly, "Spaghetti?") I wonder what it will mean for people to forget that food, like rain, is not a product but a process. I wonder how they will imagine the infinite when they have never seen how the stars fill a dark night sky. I wonder how I can explain why a wood-thrush song makes my chest hurt to a populace for whom wood is a construction material and thrush is a tongue disease. What we lose in our great human exodus from the land is a rooted sense, as deep and intangible as religious faith, of why we need to hold on to the wild and beautiful places that once surrounded us. We seem to succumb so easily to the prevailing human tendency to pave such places over, build subdivisions upon them, and name them The Willows, or Peregrine's Roost, or Elk Meadows, after whatever it was that got killed there.[33]

We need to be able to taste grace

BARBARA KINGSOLVER

Oh, how can I say this: People need wild places. Whether or not we think we do, we do. We need to be able to taste grace and know once again that we desire it.

We need to experience a landscape that is timeless, whose agenda moves at the pace of speciation and glaciers. To be surrounded by a singing, mating, howling commotion of other species, all of which love their lives as much as we do ours, and none of which could possibly care less about our economic status or our running day calendar. Wilderness puts us in our place. It reminds us that our plans are small and somewhat absurd. It reminds us why, in those cases in which our plans might influence many future generations, we ought to choose carefully. Looking out on a clean plank of planet earth, we can get shaken right down to the bone by the bronze-eyed possibility of lives that are not our own.[34]

5

All God's Creatures

The behavior of insects, birds, and other animals has long caught our attention. We watch in fascination as ants carry huge objects long distances, as the swallows return to San Juan Capistrano every March from Argentina, as kittens chase a ball of yarn, as dogs bond with families and protect human children, as mynah birds mimic human voices. Such behavior grabs our imagination for several reasons. At times we think it unbelievable or odd. At other times we watch the behavior of creatures and think it to be very human. We "anthropomorphize" creatures. After repeatedly experiencing the behavior of insects, birds, fish, and animals, we often give them human traits. They become models for our virtues or vices. Lions have courage. Owls have wisdom. Beavers are industrious. Foxes are sly. Pigs are dirty. Snakes are sneaky. These traits are often played out in literature. Fairy tales and fables illustrate the humanness of creatures. We are told to be like the slow-but-steady tortoise and not the overconfident hare.

Let's not, however, overly romanticize this point. The behavior of animals also often frightens or threatens us. Animals are a popular source of danger, from the Minotaur to the Big Bad Wolf through Moby Dick and Jaws. On the annoying scale, we've been bitten by insects, set traps for mice, and wondered where the smell of a skunk came from. It is hard to think of creatures as important elements in God's ordering of the world as we pull an embedded tick out of our leg, hold a child who has been stung by a bee, or sit in an emergency room waiting for stitches to close a dog bite. The writers of the ancient texts recognize this tension between human well-being and the behavior of creatures. The psalmist pleads to God for help from his enemies, for "like a lion they will tear me apart" and "drag me away" (Ps. 7:2). Daniel repeatedly speaks about "being thrown into the den of lions" (Dan. 6:7, 12, 16, 19, 20, 24). Jesus warns his followers: "I am sending you out like sheep into the midst of wolves; so be wise as serpents and innocent as doves. Beware of them, for they will hand you over to councils and flog you in their synagogues; and you will be dragged before governors and kings because of me" (Matt. 10:16–18).

A Sense of the Divine

Many religious themes arise in reflections on animals. People have long held that in the particular actions of creatures we can see the broader picture of God's intentions in creation. Consider the lowly earthworm. Did you know that there are 2,700 types of earthworms? Where would many of our gardens be without them aerating the soil, breaking down refuse into dirt? By looking at the diversity in creation we get a glimpse of the extent of God's creative activity. In creation we see the ordered relation between many parts. For example, in the wild, and in our own backyards, there are predators and prey. There are hawks and mice, ladybugs and aphids, and robins and earthworms doing what they are designed to do. Contemporary singer-songwriter Peter Mayer (1963–) is inspired by nature, in ways great and small, and finds the presence of the divine in a red-winged blackbird and a renewed appreciation for wild places. The bird, and nature as a whole, should not be treated as "a second-rate hand-me-down" compared to heaven, in this view.

———•◦•———

In the Bible, faith is often likened to the behavior of creatures. In being what they are, acting as they are designed, it is said that they praise God. The actions of creatures also suggest God's concern for creation. In a familiar biblical text on animals (Luke 12:24–31), Jesus

147

illustrates God's providence by pointing to the ravens and the lilies. Their continued existence and indeed their flourishing, suggests Jesus, demonstrates God's grace and care. Ravens and wild flowers are to some degree opposites. Ravens have often been thought of as noisy, raucous creatures. You do not really want a flock of them living in your backyard. Flowers, of course, provide incomparable beauty and a sense of tranquility. God provides for both. This insight ought to inspire our personal confidence in God. The birds and flowers do not worry about tomorrow. They do not have retirement plans; yet they thrive, thanks to the goodness of God.

The selections in this section include excerpts from the story of Noah and the flood in Genesis. The first narrates how Noah sends out the dove, which returns with the characteristic "olive leaf." God then announces the formation of a covenant, a solemn yet loving agreement with Noah and all living things. Later in the Bible, the prophet Hosea reaffirms the partnership with all living things in a covenant with God.

———·•·———

While we often hear the phrase "the patience of Job," Job was in fact not very patient with God. Job faces horrendous suffering and vents his frustration with God. He questions God and God responds, in part, with the text as a testimony to his knowledge, power, and providence. In the book of Numbers, God provides food for the people as they wander through the desert. Isaiah describes the chaos people in Babylon will experience because of God's wrath; wild animals run freely through the town.

⸺•⸺

Two prominent German medieval writers compare God's creatures to books. It is not surprising that Thomas à Kempis (1380–1471) uses the metaphor of the book. He was one of the most accomplished scribes of his day—that is to say, he transcribed great works in longhand. Kempis was noted for his neatness and skill, and four large volumes of his Bibles still exist. His own work, *The Imitation of Christ,* is one of the most widely published books in the Christian tradition. Meister Eckhart (1260–1327), who taught that the self-manifestation of God in the Holy Trinity was followed by his manifestation in his creatures, compares animals to words in a great book.

Speaking of books, Henry David Thoreau (1817–1862) is a classic American writer. Thoreau is most remembered for *Walden, or, A Life in the Woods,* a collection of essays he wrote while living in a small cabin on Walden Pond near Concord, Massachusetts. Thoreau was a transcendentalist. Transcendentalism was an influential literary movement in mid-nineteenth-century New England. It was not so much a philosophy as a way of viewing reality. Thoreau's writing valued simple living, personal reflection, and individualism, as it critiqued progress, worldly success, and materialism. He has been compared to John the Baptist as a prophetic voice crying in the wilderness.[1]

Hunting is an activity grounded in the wilderness. David Petersen, a former Marine helicopter pilot, teacher, and magazine editor, reflects on what it means to be a hunter, from his home in the San Juan Mountains of Colorado. In a more ordered yet still rural setting, William Least Heat Moon (1940–) writes of returning from evening prayers at the Trappist Monastery of the Holy Spirit, near Conyers, Georgia.

———•—•———

In the 1950s, Terry Tempest Williams's family was exposed to the atomic weapons testing near their home in Utah. Several family members contracted cancer. Her book *Refuge: An Unnatural History of Family and Place* is about the death of her mother, and the "place" called the Great Salt Lake. Williams (1955–) is deeply involved in policy and politics, serving on various boards and commissions and testifying before Congress on women's health and environmental issues.

Williams's activism is part of a long line of such work by writers in American history, including the ecologist Aldo Leopold. Born in Burlington, Iowa, in 1887, he studied at Yale University, worked for nearly twenty years for the U.S. Forest Service, cofounded the Wilderness Society, and taught at the University of Wisconsin until his untimely death fighting a brush fire in 1948. Leopold is best known for his book *A Sand County Almanac*, a classic collection of essays addressing what he calls "a land ethic." In his words, "a land ethic changes the role of *Homo sapiens* from conqueror of the land-community to plain member and citizen of it. It implies respect for fellow-members, and also respect for the community as such."[2] The selection here is a simple and provocative piece on the migration and value of geese.

Insects, Birds, and Animals as Symbols

Throughout the ages many creatures have been used to symbolize Jesus or aspects of Jesus's life. Jesus, for example, is the "Lamb of God." A lamb is a meek and humble creature. Its white coat symbolizes innocence and purity. In the Old Testament a lamb is the preferred animal of sacrifice. The First Letter of Peter from the New Testament captures this famously as it calls Christians to a higher level of holiness. "Therefore prepare your minds for action; discipline yourselves; set all your hope on the grace that Jesus Christ will bring you when he is revealed. . . . You know that you were ransomed from the futile ways inherited from your ancestors, not with perishable things like silver or gold, but with the precious blood of Christ, like that of a lamb without defect or blemish" (1 Peter 1:13, 18–19). Thus, ancient crucifixes often pictured a lamb above Jesus's head. Jesus often refers to himself as a shepherd and his followers as sheep. He is the Good Shepherd. This reference recalls the wonderful Psalm 23: "The Lord is my shepherd, I shall not want."

———•———

From the earliest Christian times up to today, Jesus is associated with a fish. The ancient Greek word for *fish* is formed from the first letters of the Greek phrase "Jesus Christ, God's Son, Savior." Early Christians used a drawing of a fish as a secret emblem to identify themselves to each other in times of persecution. (And one can see magnetic fish emblems stuck on the rear of automobiles—with presumably Christian drivers—today.) Jesus has other links to fish. He was a good friend of fishermen, recruited fishermen into his disciples, and indeed told them where and how to fish. The Gospels mention on several occasions that Jesus ate fish and that fish were involved in his miracles. Catholics long fasted on Fridays by avoiding meat and instead eating fish, which was considered a poor person's food; abstaining from meat was seen as a sacrifice.

Among other images, the swallow, butterfly, eagle, and pelican have been used in art in connection with Jesus. A swallow has symbolized the incarnation, Jesus becoming human. A butterfly has often been used to symbolize the resurrection of Jesus. The eagle has represented his ascension into heaven. And medieval artists have used a pelican to symbolize Jesus. Pelicans store bits of food in their large pouch under their bill. When people saw the birds picking pieces of food out of their pouches and feeding their young, they thought the pelicans were picking their own flesh and feeding their young their own blood ("this is my body, this is my blood"). Pelicans became a symbol of sacrificial love.

We see a variety of other animal symbols in the Christian tradition. A dove represents the Holy Spirit and, at the same time, peace. Ancient Christians have linked the four Gospel writers with the "four living creatures" mentioned in Revelation 4:6: "Around the throne, and on each side of the throne, are four living creatures ... the first living creature like a lion, the second living creature like an ox, the third living creature with a face like a human face, and the fourth living creature like a flying eagle." A lion symbolizes the evangelist Mark; an ox is used for Luke; a person or an angel symbolizes Matthew; and John is associated with an eagle.

———•◦•———

Several Old Testament texts suggest that animals know more than humans. The authors use irony to capture the attention of people slipping away from God. Our faith ought to be like the behavior of animals. Included here are short excerpts from the Song of Solomon, one of a very few books in the Bible that does not speak of God. The Song is a series of poems between a man and a woman in which they proclaim their mutual, exclusive, and powerful love. They embellish the beauty of each other using analogy from animals, plants, and natural wonders.

This section also includes stories about Francis of Assisi, whom we met in the second chapter. The first text recalls his conversation with a cricket and his encounter with a worm on a road. The second is his famous "Sermon to the Birds." This text is from *Little Flowers of St. Francis,* a book written in Italian about a hundred years after his death. The book contains many stories about Francis. One story has Francis, guided by the Holy Spirit, setting out with his companions on a journey to spread the Word of God. Full of enthusiasm, Francis and his companions did not even plan a route. As they walked, they happened upon a great multitude of birds. Francis told his friends to wait as he went to preach to his "little sisters the birds." As he spoke, the birds came down from the trees and surrounded him. Francis walked among them. When he finished, he blessed them and they flew out into the four directions of the earth.

There are several striking ideas in this "sermon." Francis calls the birds his "sisters." He recognizes the bond he shares with them as children of God. His words to the birds, however, are also words to us. How can birds be ungrateful? Beware the sin of ingratitude. Note that he is speaking to birds; they own nothing. Francis calls us to recognize our gifts and in gratitude use our gifts appropriately. And there is an evangelical message in this passage—the birds are asked to praise God and fly about everywhere, spreading the good news.

Modern environmental voices have been considered evangelical in the sense of a crusade, perhaps none more so for the cause of wilderness than John Muir's. Muir (1838–1914) was perhaps America's most famous preservationist. He is often referred to as "The Father of our National Parks." A writer and explorer who founded the Sierra Club, Muir influenced President Theodore Roosevelt to establish the first national monuments and Yosemite National Park.

Continuing a theme we saw in St. Francis, Francis A. Schaeffer (1912–1984) writes about the appropriate respect Christians ought to have for creatures, particularly the ant in your kitchen and the ant on your sidewalk.

Unclean Animals and Dragons

Christian readers of the Hebrew texts are often surprised to read that certain animals and food are called "unclean." Leviticus (ch. 11), for example, lists the following as unclean: camel, rock badger, pig, and creatures living in the water that have no fins and scales. The roster of birds that are not to be eaten includes eagles, vultures, and ravens. The Israelites were prohibited from eating winged insects, excepting locust and crickets. There seems to be no particular reason why some animals are on the list and others are not. Probably, however, these dietary laws were associated with a level of holiness and identity, and marked the followers off from other peoples.

If dietary laws distinguished the Israelites from other peoples, they were united by some common conceptions of the world. Excerpts from Job and Daniel mention great beasts. The beasts in Job were thought to be real, while the beasts in Daniel clearly symbolize specific kingdoms.

The images of Behemoth and Leviathan were very prevalent in the ancient Near East. Both were envisioned as powerful beasts, monsters associated with evil and chaos. Behemoth was thought of as a land creature, usually associated with a hippopotamus. That association does not, however, capture the extent of the beast's mythic destructive capacity. (Hippos, native to Africa, are herbivorous and chiefly aquatic.) Leviathan was the great sea creature, a dragon of the water, possibly a crocodile, which in Africa could grow to lengths of eighteen feet and was commonly found in the Nile River system. Leviathan, which also could have represented a whale or a serpent, appears several times in the Old Testament as well as in texts of other religions. The Hebrew texts suggest that God created both Behemoth and Leviathan and continues to keep them at bay and under control, just as God's ordering of reality keeps chaos itself at bay. God presses Job again in these sections, forcing Job to acknowledge the power of God. These creatures are under God's authority; indeed Leviathan appears to be something of God's pet!

The author of Revelation in the New Testament picks up Daniel's imagery as well as the mental pictures of Leviathan from the Old Testament. In this highly symbolic text, the devil appears as a dragon, like the symbols of evil and chaos from the earlier ages.

Holy now

PETER MAYER

This morning, outside I stood
And saw a little red-winged bird
Shining like a burning bush
Singing like a scripture verse
It made me want to bow my head
I remember when church let out
How things have changed since then

Everything is holy now
It used to be a world half there
Heaven's second-rate hand-me-down
But I walk it with a reverent air
'Cause everything is holy now.[3]

Noah sends out the dove

GENESIS 8:6–12

At the end of forty days Noah opened the window of the ark that he had made and sent out the raven; and it went to and fro until the waters were dried up from the earth. Then he sent out the dove from him, to see if the waters had subsided from the face of the ground; but the dove found no place to set its foot, and it returned to him to the ark, for the waters were still on the face of the whole earth. So he put out his hand and took it and brought it into the ark with him. He waited another seven days, and again he sent out the dove from the ark; and the dove came back to him in the evening, and there in its beak was a freshly plucked olive leaf; so Noah knew that the waters had subsided from the earth. Then he waited another seven days, and sent out the dove; and it did not return to him any more.

A covenant with all living things

GENESIS 9:8–18

Then God said to Noah and to his sons with him, "As for me, I am establishing my covenant with you and your descendants after you, and with every living creature that is with you, the birds, the domestic animals, and every animal of the earth with you, as many as came out of the ark. I establish my covenant with you, that never again shall all flesh be cut off by the waters of a flood, and never again shall there be a flood to destroy the earth." God said, "This is the sign of the covenant that I make between me and you and every living creature that is with you, for all future generations: I have set my bow in the clouds, and it shall be a sign of the covenant between me and the earth. When I bring clouds over the earth and the bow is seen in the clouds, I will remember my covenant that is between me and you and every living creature of all flesh; and the waters shall never again become a flood to destroy all flesh. When the bow is in the clouds, I will see it and remember the everlasting covenant between God and every living creature of all flesh that is on the earth."

A covenant

HOSEA 2:18

I will make for you a covenant on that day with the wild animals, the birds of the air, and the creeping things of the ground; and I will abolish the bow, the sword, and war from the land.

God puts Job in his place

JOB 39:1–3, 5–6, 9–10, 13–15, 17, 19–20, 22, 26–29

Do you know when the mountain goats give birth? Do you observe the calving of the deer? Can you number the months that they fulfill, and do you know the time when they give birth, when they crouch to give birth to their offspring, and are delivered of their young?

Who has let the wild ass go free? Who has loosed the bonds of the swift ass, to which I have given the steppe for its home, the salt land for its dwelling place?

Is the wild ox willing to serve you? Will it spend the night at your crib? Can you tie it in the furrow with ropes, or will it harrow the valleys after you?

The ostrich's wings flap wildly, though its pinions lack plumage. For it leaves its eggs to the earth, and lets them be warmed on the ground, forgetting that a foot may crush them, and that a wild animal may trample them . . . it has no fear because God has made it forget wisdom, and given it no share in understanding.

160

Do you give the horse its might? Do you clothe its neck with mane? Do you make it leap like the locust? Its majestic snorting is terrible. It paws violently, exults mightily; it goes out to meet the weapons. It laughs at fear, and is not dismayed; it does not turn back from the sword.

Is it by your wisdom that the hawk soars, and spreads its wings toward the south?

Is it at your command that the eagle mounts up and makes its nest on high? It lives on the rock and makes its home in the fastness of the rocky crag. From there it spies the prey; its eyes see it from far away.

God sends food

Numbers 11:31–32

Then a wind went out from the LORD, and it brought quails from the sea and let them fall beside the camp.... So the people worked all that day and night and all the next day, gathering the quails; the least anyone gathered was ten homers; and they spread them out for themselves all around the camp.

God's wrath

ISAIAH 13:13–14, 21–22

... I will make the heavens tremble, and the earth will be shaken out of its place, at the wrath of the LORD of hosts in the day of his fierce anger. Like a hunted gazelle, or like sheep with no one to gather them, all will turn to their own people, and all will flee to their own lands.

But wild animals will lie down there [in Babylon], and its houses will be full of howling creatures; there ostriches will live, and there goat-demons will dance. Hyenas will cry in its towers, and jackals in the pleasant palaces.

If your heart is straight with God

THOMAS À KEMPIS

If your heart is straight with God, then every creature will be to you a mirror of life and a book of holy doctrine. No creature is so little or so mean as not to show forth and represent the goodness of God.[4]

Every creature is a word of God

MEISTER ECKHART

Apprehend God in all things, for God is in all things. Every single creature is full of God and is a book about God. Every creature is a word of God. If I spent enough time with the tiniest creature—even a caterpillar—I would never have to prepare a sermon. So full of God is every creature.[5]

Notice the ravens

LUKE 12:24–28

Consider the ravens: they neither sow nor reap, they have neither storehouse nor barn, and yet God feeds them. Of how much more value are you than the birds! And can any of you by worrying add a single hour to your span of life? If then you are not able to do so small a thing as that, why do you worry about the rest? Consider the lilies, how they grow: they neither toil nor spin; yet I tell you, even Solomon in all his glory was not clothed like one of these. But if God so clothes the grass of the field, which is alive today and tomorrow is thrown into the oven, how much more will he clothe you—you of little faith!

Resurrection

HENRY DAVID THOREAU

Every one has heard the story which has gone the rounds of New England, of a strong and beautiful bug which came out of the dry leaf of an old table of apple-tree wood, which had stood in a farmer's kitchen for sixty years, first in Connecticut, and afterward in Massachusetts,—from an egg deposited in the living tree many years earlier still, as appeared by counting the annual layers beyond it; which was heard gnawing out for several weeks, hatched perchance by the heat of an urn. Who does not feel his faith in a resurrection and immortality strengthened by hearing of this?[6]

Hunting for spirituality

David Petersen

What I bring to the hunt is a visceral desire to play my naturally evolved, ecologically sound, and (therefore) naturally moral role as an active participant in the most intimate workings of wild nature. I want to live, as far as possible, the way humans are meant to live. I want to nourish my body with clean, lean, wild meat, the food that made us human. And I want the palpably spiritual bonding with Earth and the great round of life and death and sacramental (as opposed to commercial) trophism that, for myself and so many others, only hunting can provide. When I get out there and get slowed down and tuned in enough to perceive and appreciate even the subtlest elements of natural creation—a warm mosaic of lichen on cold granite, a velvety fuzz of moss on a rotting log, the symphonic purling of a mountain stream, the sight and sound of one leaf falling—when I've got that good old "savage" connection going, I'm absolutely aglow with the joy of life, and unafraid of death. Without the intercession of clergy, shaman, or psychotropic drug, I have stepped through the cultural wall and into a primordially sacred realm. I have entered heaven on Earth.[7]

Sounds of night

WILLIAM LEAST HEAT MOON

Afterwards, I returned to the balcony. Empty but for the sounds of dusk coming on: tree frogs, whippoorwills, crickets. I've read that Hindus count three hundred thirty million gods. Their point isn't the accuracy of the count but rather the multiplicity of the godhead. That night, if you listened, it seemed everywhere. I sat staring and felt "strong upon me," as Whitman has it, "that life does not exhibit itself." Someone behind, someone tall, said my name.[8]

Spirit life

TERRY TEMPEST WILLIAMS

I was raised to believe in a spirit world, that life exists before earth and will continue to exist afterward, that each human being, bird and bulrush, along with all other life forms had a spirit life before it came to dwell physically on the earth. Each occupied an assigned sphere of influence, each has a place and a purpose.

It made sense to a child. And if the natural world was assigned spiritual values, then those days spent in the wilderness were sacred. We learned at an early age that God can be found wherever you are, especially outside. Family worship was not just relegated to Sunday in a chapel.[9]

Epic journey

Aldo Leopold

My notes tell me I have seen a thousand geese this fall. Every one of these in the course of their epic journey from the arctic to the gulf has on one occasion or another probably served man in some equivalent of paid entertainment. One flock perhaps has thrilled a score of schoolboys, and sent them scurrying home with tales of high adventure. Another, passing overhead of a dark night, has serenaded a whole city with goose music, and awakened who knows what questionings and memories and hopes. A third perhaps has given pause to some farmer at his plow, and brought new thoughts of far lands and journeyings and peoples, where before was only drudgery, barren of any thought at all. I am sure those thousand geese are paying human dividends on a dollar value. Worth in dollars is only an exchange value, like the sale value of a painting or the copyright of a poem. What about the replacement value? Supposing there were no longer any painting, or poetry, or goose music? It is a black thought to dwell upon, but it must be answered. In dire necessity somebody might write another *Iliad*, or paint an "Angelus," but fashion a goose? "I, the Lord, will answer them. The hand of the Lord hath done this, and the Holy One of Israel created it."

I heard of a boy who was brought up an athcist. He changed his mind when he saw that there were a hundrcd-odd species of warblers, each bedecked like to the rainbow, and each performing yearly sundry thousands of miles of migration about which scientists wrote wisely but did not understand. No "fortuitous concourse of elements" working blindly through any number of millions of years could quite account for why warblers are so beautiful. No mechanistic theory, even bolstered by mutations, has ever quite answered for the colors of the cerulean warbler, or the vespers of the wood thrush, or the swansong, or—goose music. I dare say this boy's convictions would be harder to shake than those of many inductive theologians. There are yet many boys to be born who, like Isaiah, "may see, and know, and consider, and understand together, that the hand of the Lord hath done this." But where shall they see, and know, and consider? In museums?[10]

Animals know more than we I

ISAIAH 1:3

The ox knows its owner, and the donkey its master's crib; but Israel does not know, my people do not understand.

Animals know more than we II

JOB 12:7–10

But ask the animals, and they will teach you; the birds of the air, and they will tell you; ask the plants of the earth, and they will teach you; and the fish of the sea will declare to you. Who among all these does not know that the hand of the LORD has done this? In his hand is the life of every living thing and the breath of every human being.

Animals know more than we III

JEREMIAH 8:7

Even the stork in the heavens knows its times; and the turtledove, swallow, and crane observe the time of their coming; but my people do not know the ordinance of the LORD.

Virtuous creatures

PROVERBS 30:24–33

Four things on earth are small, yet they are exceedingly wise: the ants are a people without strength, yet they provide their food in the summer; the badgers are a people without power, yet they make their homes in the rocks; the locusts have no king, yet all of them march in rank; the lizard can be grasped in the hand, yet it is found in kings' palaces.

Three things are stately in their stride; four are stately in their gait: the lion, which is mightiest among wild animals and does not turn back before any; the strutting rooster, the he-goat, and a king striding before his people.

If you have been foolish, exalting yourself, or if you have been devising evil, put your hand on your mouth. For as pressing milk produces curds, and pressing the nose produces blood, so pressing anger produces strife.

Like a deer I

PSALM 42:1

As a deer longs for flowing streams, so my soul longs for you, O God.

Like a deer II

Habakkuk 3:19

God, the Lord, is my strength; he makes my feet like the feet of a deer, and makes me tread upon the heights.

The wolf and the lamb, the calf and the lion

Isaiah 11:6–9

The wolf shall live with the lamb, the leopard shall lie down with the kid, the calf and the lion and the fatling together, and a little child shall lead them. The cow and the bear shall graze, their young shall lie down together; and the lion shall eat straw like the ox. The nursing child shall play over the hole of the asp, and the weaned child shall put its hand on the adder's den. They will not hurt or destroy on all my holy mountain; for the earth will be full of the knowledge of the Lord as the waters cover the sea.

Love story I: he calls out to her

Song of Solomon 1:9, 15; 4:1, 2, 5

I compare you, my love, to a mare among Pharaoh's chariots.

Ah, you are beautiful, my love; ah, you are beautiful; your eyes are doves.

Your hair is like a flock of goats . . . your teeth are like
a flock of shorn ewes . . . your two breasts are like two
fawns.

Love story II: she calls out to him

SONG OF SOLOMON 2:9, 15; 5:11–12

My beloved is like a gazelle or a young stag.
Catch us the foxes, the little foxes.
His head is the finest gold; his locks are wavy, black
as a raven. His eyes are like doves.

Sister Cricket and little worms

THOMAS OF CELANO

One time during summer blessed Francis was at that
same place, and he stayed in the last cell next to the
hedge of the garden behind the house. . . . It happened
that one day, as he came down from that little cell, there
was a cricket within on the branch of the fig tree next
to that cell, and he could touch it. Stretching out his
hand, he said: "Sister Cricket, come to me." The cricket
immediately climbed onto the fingers of his hand, and
with a finger of his other hand, he began to touch it, saying, "Sing, my Sister Cricket." It obeyed him at once and
began to chirp. This consoled blessed Francis greatly and
he praised God. He held it in his hand that way for more

171

than an hour. Afterwards he put it back on the branch of the fig tree from which he had taken it.[11]

Blessed Francis found so much joy in creatures because of love of the Creator, to console him in his inner and outer self, that the Lord made even those that are wild to people become tame to him.

Even for worms he had a warm love, since he had read this text about the Savior: "I am a worm and not a man." That is why he used to pick them up from the road and put them in a safe place so that they would not be crushed by the footsteps of passersby.

What shall I say about the other lesser creatures? In the winter he had honey or the best wine put out for the bees so that they would not perish from the cold. He used to extol the artistry of their work and their remarkable ingenuity, giving glory to the Lord.

How great do you think was the delight the beauty of flowers brought to his soul whenever he saw their lovely form and noticed their sweet fragrance? He would immediately turn his gaze to the beauty of that flower, brilliant in the springtime, sprouting "from the root of Jesse." . . . Whenever he found an abundance of flowers, he used to preach to them and invite them to praise the Lord, just as if they were endowed with reason.[12]

Sermon to the birds

St. Francis of Assisi

My little Sisters, the birds, you are such beloved by God, your creator, and in every place you should praise him with your song. Remember that he has doubly and even triply dressed you and you can go where you wish. He saved your species in the ark of Noah so that you would not be lost to the world. You should also be thankful for the sustenance of the air, which God has given you as your province. Beyond that, you do not have to plant or harvest. God gives you food to eat and provides springs and rivers for when you are thirsty; there are hills and valleys for your refuge and trees to make your nests. You do not have to sow or weave, for God gives you and your offspring ample clothing. So love your creator, for he has done so much for you. Finally, my little sisters, beware of the sin of ingratitude. Be ready always to give praises and thank God.[13]

Honor the ant

Francis A. Schaeffer

Christians, of all people, should not be destroyers. We should treat nature with an overwhelming respect. We may cut down a tree to build a house, or to make a fire to keep the family warm. But we should not cut down the tree just to cut down the tree. We may, if necessary, bark the cork tree in order to have the use of the bark. But what we should not do is to bark the tree simply for the sake of doing so, and let it dry and stand there a dead skeleton in the wind. To do so is not to treat the tree with integrity. We have the right to rid our houses of ants; but what we have no right to do is to forget to honor the ant as God made it, out in the place where God made the ant to be. When we meet the ant on the sidewalk, we step over him. He is a creature, like ourselves; not made in the image of God, it is true, but equal with man as far as creation is concerned. The ant and the man are both creatures.[14]

God's family

JOHN MUIR

How narrow we selfish, conceited creatures are in our sympathies! How blind to the rights of all the rest of creation! With what dismal irreverence we speak of our fellow mortals! Though alligators, snakes, etc., naturally repel us, they are not mysterious evils. They dwell happily in these flowery wilds, are part of God's family, unfallen, undepraved, and cared for with the same species of tenderness and love as is bestowed on angels in heaven or saints on earth.[15]

The great beast

JOB 40:15–24

"Look at Behemoth, which I made just as I made you; it eats grass like an ox. Its strength is in its loins, and its power in the muscles of its belly. It makes its tail stiff like a cedar; the sinews of its thighs are knit together. Its bones are tubes of bronze, its limbs like bars of iron. It is the first of the great acts of God—only its Maker can approach it with the sword. For the mountains yield food for it where all the wild animals play. Under the lotus plants it lies, in the covert of the reeds and in the marsh. The lotus trees cover it for shade; the willows of the wadi [valley] surround it. Even if the river is turbulent, it is not frightened; it is confident though Jordan rushes against its mouth. Can one take it with hooks or pierce its nose with a snare?"

The great sea monster

JOB 41:1–8

"Can you draw out Leviathan with a fishhook, or press down its tongue with a cord? Can you put a rope in its nose, or pierce its jaw with a hook? Will it make many supplications to you? Will it speak soft words to you? Will it make a covenant with you to be taken as your servant forever? Will you play with it as with a bird, or will you put it on leash for your girls? Will traders bargain over it? Will they divide it up among the merchants? Can you fill its skin with harpoons, or its head with fishing spears? Lay hands on it; think of the battle; you will not do it again!"

The vision of the four beasts

DANIEL 7:1–8; 15–18

In the first year of King Belshazzar of Babylon, Daniel had a dream and visions of his head as he lay in bed. Then he wrote down the dream: I, Daniel, saw in my vision by night the four winds of heaven stirring up the great sea, and four great beasts came up out of the sea, different from one another. The first was like a lion and had eagles' wings. Then, as I watched, its wings were plucked off, and it was lifted up from the ground and made to stand on two feet like a human being; and a human mind was given to it. Another beast appeared, a second one, that looked like a bear. It was raised up on one side, had three tusks in its mouth among its teeth and was told, "Arise, devour many bodies!" After this, as I watched, another appeared, like a leopard. The beast had four wings of a bird on its back and four heads; and dominion was given to it. After this I saw in the visions by night a fourth beast, terrifying and dreadful and exceedingly strong. It had great iron teeth and was devouring, breaking in pieces, and stamping what was left with its feet. It was different from all the beasts that preceded it, and it had ten horns. I was considering the horns, when another horn appeared, a little one coming up among them; to make room for it, three of the earlier horns were plucked up by the roots. There were eyes like human eyes in this horn, and a mouth speaking arrogantly . . .

As for me, Daniel, my spirit was troubled within me, and the visions of my head terrified me. I approached one of the attendants to ask him the truth concerning all this. So he said that he would disclose to me the interpretation of the matter: "As for these four great beasts, four kings shall arise out of the earth. But the holy ones of the Most High shall receive the kingdom and possess the kingdom forever—forever and ever."

Satan as a serpent

REVELATION 12:1–9

A great portent appeared in heaven: a woman clothed with the sun, with the moon under her feet, and on her head a crown of twelve stars. She was pregnant and was crying out in birth pangs, in the agony of giving birth. Then another portent appeared in heaven: a great red dragon, with seven heads and ten horns, and seven diadems on his heads. His tail swept down a third of the stars of heaven and threw them to the earth. Then the dragon stood before the woman who was about to bear a child, so that he might devour her child as soon as it was born. And she gave birth to a son, a male child, who is to rule all the nations with a rod of iron. But her child was snatched away and taken to God and to his throne; and the woman fled into the wilderness, where she has a place prepared by God, so that there she can be nourished for one thousand two hundred sixty days.

And war broke out in heaven; Michael and his angels fought against the dragon. The dragon and his angels fought back, but they were defeated, and there was no longer any place for them in heaven. The great dragon was thrown down, that ancient serpent, who is called the Devil and Satan, the deceiver of the whole world—he was thrown down to the earth, and his angels were thrown down with him.

Conclusion

The language of religious experience is difficult to enter. Christians through the ages have wrestled with this. Some testify to strong, life-changing moments when God is felt as a direct presence. Others experience God in a low-key fashion. Instead of experiencing a flash of lightning, instead of being knocked off a horse, they perceive God in less direct, more subtle senses. On either account, knowledge of God is mediated through particular experiences. We get a sense of God through contact with others, in religious services, rituals, prayers, and, as this book has suggested, through interaction with nature.

What is it about nature that does this? A walk in the woods, a canoe ride down a river, a camping trip, fishing on a quiet lake, sitting on a rock by the shore, crouching in a duck blind, hours spent tending a garden in the backyard—all such experiences can be avenues that spark a sense of the divine in our lives. To put it simply, experiences in and of nature can evoke basic religious feelings.

Scholars have described several distinctive religious feelings or senses.[1] These senses can be directly related to the outdoors experiences listed above. A primary, perhaps *the* primary, religious feeling is a sense of dependence. Experiences in nature often evoke such feelings. In some significant ways, we are not unlike a tree in the forest, a plant in the yard, or a fish in a lake. We, like the tree, flower, and fish, need nourishment and a safe, healthy environment to survive and to flourish. Our well-being is, to a great extent, dependent on the activity of others. Although we are autonomous individuals, we rely on others; or, perhaps better stated, we all are interdependent.

As a good trip often "depends" on the weather, so too a good life "depends" on the complex interactions of one life with others. We live in a vast and dynamic world not of our own making. Encounters with nature stir our sense of being limited and finite. They also can encourage us to consider our connectedness with others and the world and our ultimate dependence on God. A sense of gratitude often follows as one appreciates his or her dependence and interdependence. Our encounters with nature can encourage the sense that these things are good and that our God is good. We are then thankful for calm, sunny days, gentle breezes at dusk, and the sounds of the earth waking up. Thankfulness is a basic religious response to life.

Thankfulness, however, ought not merely be a resting place. It is a call to responsibility and to action. We often have to nourish the conditions and work on the friendships to continue the relationships. Group camping, hiking, and canoe trips for young people are often specifically organized to develop these senses in participants. Leaders want their charges to feel a part of a team, part of a project that is bigger than themselves. They want their students to feel that they are vital parts of a greater whole, and that they depend on other group members and that others depend on them. Group campers come to appreciate the efforts of others and hope that others recognize their contributions. Any leader would tell you that the success of such a trip is measured not merely by everyone doing his or her task but by a gradual personalization and "ownership" of each task by those involved. Kids, for example, recognize their responsibilities and take pride in their work. On a larger scale, many people become conservationists or environmentalists because of a keen, well-developed sense of responsibility that comes from time in the wilderness spent fishing, hunting, hiking, or biking. One thinks of the pioneer environmentalist John Muir's famous "thousand-mile walk" from the Midwest to the Gulf of Mexico and his conversion.

Like wilderness, religious senses and feelings are not all "warm and fuzzy." With an honest awareness of dependence, recognition, gratitude, and a heightened sense of responsibility comes another basic religious sense. It is the realization that one is not always living as one should be living. True religious experiences often include a sense of conversion or change. Lives are transformed. Sometimes our rational or intellectual side is tested. We must think about the use and overuse of resources. One objective of this book is to assist the reader in a transformation; it is to engage the reader's head and heart in a spiritual relationship with nature.

There are at least two other basic religious feelings or senses that can arise from reflecting on our time in the woods. They are hope and purpose. You have heard this line before: "If you have done that [camped for a week in the rain, hiked for a day up the side of a mountain ... insert any vigorous challenge here], you can do anything you set your mind to!" Hope as a renewed sense of possibility is often engendered by contacts with creation. The increased mental space afforded in such experiences can be an opportunity to broaden our vision. Meeting challenges can boast our self-confidence.

With hope can come a new or refreshed sense of purpose. The experience of many suggests that hours spent away from cell phones and televisions and traffic jams offers occasion to consider vital questions. One can clear one's mind with a nice walk through the woods. In a phrase often attributed to President Herbert Hoover, a dedicated fly-fisherman, "God does not subtract from man's allotted time on Earth the hours spent fishing." All of this is to say that such periods offer opportunities to reaffirm or reconsider the direction of one's life.

Jesus often went to the sea, up the mountain, or into the desert. Nature was a way through which he entered into prayer and sensed the divine on earth. Each of us would do well to do the same. We hope this book helps as you go on your way.

Notes

Introduction

1. Herman Melville, *Moby Dick, or, The Whale* (New York: Penguin, 1999), 4.

2. As reprinted in *By the Light of the Glow-Worm Lamp: Three Centuries on Reflections of Nature*, ed. Alberto Manguel (New York: Plenum, 1998), 61.

3. Robert Chambers, *Vestiges of the Natural History of Creation and Other Evolutionary Writings*, ed. James A. Secord (Chicago: University of Chicago Press, 1994). Originally published in 1844.

4. Kenneth R. Miller, *Finding Darwin's God* (New York: HarperCollins, 1999), 283.

5. Flannery O'Connor, *The Habit of Being: Letters of Flannery O'Connor* (New York: Farrar, Straus and Giroux, 1979), 128.

6. Luke Dysinger, "The Practice of *Lectio Divina*," in *An Invitation to Centering Prayer*, by M. Basil Pennington (Liguori, MI: Liguori, 2001), 49–50.

7. Sigurd Olson, *Listening Point* (New York: Knopf, 1989), 3.

8. Ibid., 8.

9. Dysinger, "The Practice of *Lectio Divina*," 50.

10. Ibid., 51.

Chapter 1: On Creation and the Creator

1. Wendell Berry, "Christianity and the Survival of Creation," *Cross Currents* 43, no. 2 (summer 1993): 149.

2. From *Webster's 1913 Dictionary* under "wisdom." As referenced in www .hyperdictionary.com/dictionary/wisdom.

3. Izaak Walton, *The Compleat Angler* (London: Oxford University Press, 1921), 37–38. Originally published in 1653.

4. Daniel Defoe, *Robinson Crusoe* (New York: Norton, 1975), 15ff. Originally published in 1719.

5. See for example 1 Timothy 6:13 or 2 Corinthians 9:13.

6. Augustine, "Sermon 68.6," in *Sermons (51–94) on the New Testament,* ed. John Rotelle (New York: New City Press, 1991).

7. Sometimes attributed to Pope Gregory the Great.

8. Berry, "Christianity and the Survival of Creation," 149.

9. Augustine, *The City of God,* trans. R. W. Dyson (Cambridge: Cambridge University Press, 1998), book 22, chapter 24.

10. Thomas Aquinas, *Summa Theologica* (New York: Benzinger Brothers, 1947), I, Q. 47, art. 1.

11. Thomas Traherne in *Mysticism: A Study and an Anthology,* by F. C. Happold (New York: Penguin, 1970), 371–72.

12. Augustine, "Sermon 68.6."

13. Thérèse of Lisieux, trans. John Clark, *Story of a Soul: The Autobiography of Saint Thérèse of Lisieux* (Washington, DC: ICS Publications, 1996), 14.

14. Augustine, "Sermon 241," in *Sermons 230–272B,* ed. John E. Rotelle (New York: New City Press, 1993).

15. Julian of Norwich, *Revelations of Divine Love,* trans. Elizabeth Spearing (London: Penguin, 1998), 54, 89.

16. Ibid., 47.

17. Edgar D. Mitchell, "Outer Space to Inner Space: An Astronaut's Journey," in *Saturday Review,* February 22, 1975: 20.

18. James Irwin, quoted in M. Dows, *Earthspirit: A Handbook for Nurturing an Ecological Christianity* (Mystic, CT: Twenty-third Publications, 1990), 94.

19. Eugene Cernan, quoted in Frank White, *Overview Effect* (Boston: American Institute of Aeronautics and Astronautics, 1987), 39.

20. Wendell Berry, "The Journey's End," in *Words from the Land*, ed. Stephen Trimble (Las Vegas: University of Nevada Press, 1995), 236.

Chapter 2: Our Place in Creation

1. See James Gustafson, *A Sense of the Divine: The Natural Environment from a Theocentric Perspective* (Cleveland: Pilgrim Press, 1994).

2. Ludwig Bieler, *The Patrician Texts in the Book of Armagh* (Dublin: Dublin Institute for Advanced Studies, 1979), 143.

3. Steven Bouma-Prediger, *For the Beauty of the Earth: A Christian Vision for Creation Care* (Grand Rapids: Baker Academic, 2001), 14.

4. Thomas McDowell, ed., *Thomas Merton Reader* (Garden City, NY: Image Books, 1974), 504.

5. Adopted by the General Board of the American Baptist Churches, June 1989. See www.abc-usa.org/resources/resol/ecology.htm.

6. Evangelical Environmental Network. See www.creationcare.org.

7. John Paul II, from Lorenzago Dicardore, Italy, discussing hiking in the Dolomite Mountains, July 15, 1996, and homily in Val Visdene, Italy, on the Feast Day of St. John Gualbert, Patron of Foresters, 1990. See conservation.catholic.org/pope_john_paul_ii.htm.

8. Evangelical Lutheran Church in America, "Caring for Creation: Vision, Hope, and Justice," August 28, 1993. See www.elca.org/dcs/environment.html.

9. United Nations Environment Programme, "Only One Earth" (New York: United Nations, 1990). This was published for "Environmental Sabbath/Earth Rest Day," June 1990.

10. Ibid.

11. Text compiled from a variety of sources.

12. Translation from United States Catholic Conference.

13. Ted Perry, "Chief Seattle's Message," in *A Peace Reader: Essential Readings on War, Justice, Non-Violence, and World Order*, ed. Joseph Fahey and Richard Armstrong (New York: Paulist Press, 1992), 153.

14. Fyodor Dostoyevsky, *The Brothers Karamazov*, ed. Ralph Matlaw (New York: W. W. Norton, 1976), 298, 301.

15. Pierre Teilhard de Chardin, *The Divine Milieu: An Essay on the Interior Life* (New York: Harper and Row, 1968), 112; and *Toward the Future* (New York: Harcourt Brace Jovanovich, 1975), 72.

16. Ambrose of Milan, *On Naboth* 2, 11, 53, in *Message of the Fathers of the Church, 20: Social Thought,* by Peter Phan (Wilmington, DE: Michael Glazier, 1984).

17. Translation from Roger T. Ames and Henry Rosemont Jr., eds., *The Analects of Confucius* (New York: Ballantine, 1998), 90.

18. Translation from Arthur Waley, ed., *Lao Tzu: Tao te ching* (Ware, UK: Wordsworth, 1997), 8.

Chapter 3: That Special Spot

1. See W. Scott Olsen and Scott Cairns, eds., *The Sacred Place: Witnessing the Holy in the Physical World* (Salt Lake City: University of Utah Press, 1996).

2. See Ian Bradley, *The Celtic Way* (London: Darton, Longman and Todd, 1993), 31–50.

3. Bernard of Clairvaux, *Life and Works of St. Bernard, Abbott of Clairvaux,* ed. and trans. Samuel Eales (London: John Hodges, 1889), 2:461.

4. Sigurd Olson, *The Meaning of Wilderness: Essential Articles and Speeches,* ed. David Backes (Minneapolis: University of Minnesota Press, 2001), 135, 144.

5. See David Backes, *A Wilderness Within* (Minneapolis: University of Minnesota Press, 1999).

6. Edward Abbey, *Desert Solitaire* (Tucson: University of Arizona Press, 1968 [1988 ed.]), 247.

7. James Silas Rogers, "Roads, Stories, Indians, Air," unpublished essay, 2004.

8. See John Baumann, "The Emergence of Religion and Ecology," *Council of Societies for the Study of Religion Bulletin* 32, no. 3 (November 2003).

9. See for example Belden C. Lane, *Landscapes of the Sacred: Geography and Narrative in American Spirituality* (Baltimore: Johns Hopkins, 2001).

10. William S. Skylstad, "Waters of Life," *America Magazine*, November 23, 2003: 13.

11. Tim Robinson, *Setting Foot on the Shores of Connemara & Other Writings* (Dublin: Lilliput Press, 1996), 163–64.

12. Aldo Leopold, *A Sand County Almanac* (New York: Oxford, 1949), 137.

13. Alcuin in Ludwig Bieler, *Ireland, Harbinger of the Middle Ages* (London: Oxford University Press, 1963), 59.

14. Bernard of Clairvaux, *Life and Works*, 2:464.

15. Abbey, *Desert Solitaire*, 58.

16. Sigurd Olson, *Reflections from the North Country* (New York: Knopf, 1976), 27–29.

17. Thomas P. McDonnell, ed., *Through the Year with Thomas Merton: Daily Meditations from His Writings* (Garden City, NY: Image, 1985), 59.

18. Mother Teresa of Calcutta, *A Gift for God: Prayers and Meditations* (San Francisco: Harper and Row, 1975), 68–69.

19. Canadian Conference of Catholic Bishops, "A Pastoral Letter on the Christian Ecological Imperative," #15, www.cccb.ca/Files/pastoralenvironment.html.

20. Annie Dillard, *Pilgrim at Tinker Creek* (New York: Harper's Magazine Press, 1974), 76.

21. Ibid., 2–3.

22. Annie Dillard, *Teaching a Stone to Talk: Expeditions and Encounters* (New York: Harper and Row, 1982), 15.

23. Rogers, "Roads, Stories, Indians, Air."

24. Pierre Teilhard de Chardin, *Hymn of the Universe* (New York: Harper and Row, 1961), 68–69.

25. Edward Conze, trans., *Buddhist Scriptures* (New York: Penguin, 1959), 63–64.

26. Burton Watson, trans., *Chuang Tzu: Basic Writings* (New York: Columbia University Press, 1996), 97.

27. Richard Jefferies in Happold, *Mysticism*, 354–56.

28. John Neihardt, *Black Elk Speaks: Being the Life Story of a Holy Man of the Oglala Sioux* (Lincoln: University of Nebraska Press, 1993), 43.

29. John Paul II, discussing hiking in the Dolomite Mountains, 15 July 1996. See conservation.catholic.org/pope_john_paul_ii.htm.

30. Annie Dillard, *Holy the Firm* (New York: Harper, 1977), 19–20.

31. Norman Richardson, *The Pilgrim, the Island, and the Dove: A Story of Saint Columba* (Belfast: Corrymeela Press, 1997), 20.

Chapter 4: Into the Wilderness

1. Walter Isaacson, *Benjamin Franklin: An American Life* (New York: Simon and Schuster, 2003), 316.

2. James Nash, *Loving Nature: Ecological Integrity and Christian Responsibility* (Nashville: Abingdon, 1991), 114.

3. David R. Williams, *Wilderness Lost: The Religious Origins of the American Mind* (Selinsgrove, PA: Susquehanna University Press, 1987), 25.

4. Ulrich Mauser, *Christ in the Wilderness* (Naperville, IL: Alec R. Allenson, 1963), 21.

5. Amber Mason, "Scholars of Solitude," *University of Chicago Magazine* 96, no. 2 (December 2003): 31.

6. Ibid.

7. Ibid.

8. David Roberts, *Moments of Doubt* (Seattle: The Mountaineers, 1986), 187.

9. Ibid., 215.

10. Olson, *Reflections from the North Country,* 149.

11. John Haines, *The Stars, the Snow, the Fire* (St. Paul: Graywolf, 2000), x.

12. As quoted in David Baron, *The Beast in the Garden* (New York: Norton, 2003), 239.

13. Stewart Herman, "The Spirituality of Travel: Seekers and Satisfiers," unpublished essay, 2003.

14. Alban Butler, *Lives of the Saints,* ed. Herbert Thurston and Donald Attwater (New York: P. J. Kenedy and Sons, 1956), 2:328.

15. George Little, *Brendan the Navigator* (Dublin: M. H. Gill and Sons, 1946), 68.

16. Barry Lopez, *Arctic Dreams* (New York: Charles Scribner's Sons, 1986), 354.

17. Robert Pirsig, *Zen and the Art of Motorcycle Maintenance,* as quoted in Paul Loeb, *Soul of a Citizen* (New York: St. Martin's Griffin, 1999), 317.

18. Obituary, Florence Curl Jones, Associated Press wire, November 30, 2003.

19. Olson, *Reflections from the North Country*, 35.

20. Ibid., 1.

21. Ibid., 29–31.

22. Haines, *The Stars, the Snow, the Fire*, 36.

23. Martin Luther, *Works*, vol. 1, *Lectures on Genesis, Chapters 1–5*, ed. Jaroslav Pelikan (St. Louis: Concordia Publishing House, 1958), 64.

24. Ibid., 77.

25. Ibid., 78.

26. Ibid., 64.

27. Ibid., 208.

28. Anne Bradstreet, *Meditations Divine and Moral* (1664/1867), reprinted in *Reading the Roots: American Nature Writing before Walden*, ed. Michael P. Branch (Athens: University of Georgia Press, 2004), 69.

29. Cotton Mather, *Of Comets*, reprinted in Branch, *Reading the Roots*, 113.

30. Gene Stratton Porter, *Coming through the Swamp: The Nature Writings of Gene Stratton Porter* (Salt Lake City: University of Utah Press, 1996), 112.

31. Gretel Ehrlich, "On Water," in *Words from the Land*, ed. Stephen Trimble (Las Vegas: University of Nevada Press, 1995), 205–6.

32. Pope John Paul II, Angelus in the Apennines, 1993. See conservation .catholic.org/pope_john_paul_ii.htm.

33. Barbara Kingsolver, *Small Wonder: Essays* (New York: HarperCollins, 2002), 66–67.

34. Barbara Kingsolver, in *America 24/7*, ed. Rick Smolan and David Elliot Cohen (London: DK, 2003), 264.

Chapter 5: All God's Creatures

1. Basil Willey, Introduction, in Henry David Thoreau, *Walden* (New York: Bramhall House, 1951), 12, 16.

2. Leopold, *Sand County Almanac*, 240.

3. Peter Mayer, "Holy Now," *Million-Year Mind* (St. Paul: Blueboat Records BB1204, 1999).

4. Thomas à Kempis, *The Imitation of Christ*, ed. Harold Gardiner (Garden City, NY: Image, 1955), 80.

5. Matthew Fox, ed., *Meditations with Meister Eckhart* (Santa Fe: Bear & Co., 1982), 14.

6. Thoreau, *Walden*, 353–54.

7. David Petersen, "Hunting for Spirituality: An Oxymoron?" in *The Good in Nature and Humanity: Connecting Science, Religion, and Spirituality with the Natural World*, ed. Stephen R. Kellert and Timothy J. Farnham (Washington, DC: Island Press, 2002), 184.

8. William Least Heat Moon, *Blue Highways* (Boston: Little, Brown, 1982), 83.

9. Terry Tempest Williams, *Refuge: An Unnatural History of Family and Place* (New York: Random House, 1991), 14.

10. Leopold, *Sand County Almanac*, 230–32.

11. "The Assisi Compilation," 110 in *Francis of Assisi: Early Documents*, vol. 2, *The Founder*, ed. Regis Armstrong, J. A. Wayne Hellmann, William Short (New York: New City Press, 2000), 217, 218.

12. Thomas of Celano, *The Life of Saint Francis*, book 1, chapter 29 in *Francis of Assisi: Early Documents*, vol. 1, *The Saint*, ed. Regis Armstrong, J. A. Wayne Hellmann, William Short (New York: New City Press, 1999), 250, 251.

13. Lawrence Cunningham, ed., *Brother Francis: An Anthology of Writings by and about St. Francis of Assisi* (San Francisco: Harper and Row, 1972), 73.

14. Francis A. Schaeffer, *Pollution and the Death of Man* (Wheaton, IL: Tyndale, 1970), 74–75.

15. John Muir, *A Thousand-Mile Walk to the Gulf* (Boston: Houghton Mifflin, 1916), 98–99.

Conclusion

1. See James Gustafson, *Can Ethics Be Christian?* (Chicago: University of Chicago Press, 1975), 100–114, and *Ethics from a Theocentric Perspective*, vol. 1, *Theology and Ethics* (Chicago: University of Chicago Press, 1981), 129–34.